ENCOUNTERS
--- WITH ---
WISDOM

ENCOUNTERS
--- WITH ---
WISDOM

BOOK SEVEN

Thomas Hora, M. D.

The PAGL Foundation
www.pagl.org

Published by the PAGL Foundation
www.pagl.org
The PAGL Foundation
c/o Robert Wieser
14 Hidden Brook Road
Riverside, CT 06878

Manufactured in the United States of America.
ISBN: 978-0-913105-25-2

Contents

Editors' Preface

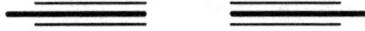

This book presents dialogues between Dr. Thomas Hora, psychiatrist, spiritual teacher, and founder of Existential Metapsychiatry, and some of his students. They occurred in the late 1980s through 1995. Dr. Hora recorded most of the group sessions with his students, and made them available to those whoattended. The PAGL Foundation[1] has collected many of these tapes and transcribed them. For the reader new to the teachings of Metapsychiatry, it is suggested that these dialogues will be more meaningful if one of Dr. Hora's other books, especially *Beyond the Dream*, is read first.

Dr. Hora maintained his practice in his homes (an apartment in New York City and a house in Bedford, New York). Group sessions were held in the living room, where chairs were arranged in a circle. After the students had gathered, Dr. Hora would enter and sit down. He greeted each student non-verbally with eye contact and a smile, and then he waited for a question to be asked. If no question was forthcoming, Dr. Hora opened the dialogue.

Metapsychiatry values the sincere question, and Dr. Hora always waited for students to formulate questions. He listened for their sincerity as this indicated a student's receptivity and desire to understand. Sometimes a question might be phrasedin an awkward or convoluted way. In such instances some of the meandering has been edited here for the sake of clarity.

---

1 - PAGL is an acronym for Peace, Assurance, Gratitude, and Love, qualities of consciousness that are the fruit of spiritual understanding. The PAGL Foundation was established to make Dr. Hora's work available (see *www.PAGL.org*).

As a dialogue progressed, there could be long silences or pauses. At such times Dr. Hora might introduce an entirely new topic, perhaps discerning an unasked question. He also saw and was amused by the paradoxes that life offered, and often shared this in asides and humorous remarks. He showed his students how to laugh at their woes by lifting their vision to a higher perspective, helping them make the distinction between taking something seriously vs. giving it full attention. Laughter erupted frequently.

Overall, the editors have chosen to keep the flow of the dialogue as it occurred, so that no major changes have been made other than to maintain the anonymity of the participants and improve readability. Although some of the ideas in these dialogues may have been addressed in various ways in other available materials, to the sincere student, the freshness of these sessions can offer new insights and reinforce old ones.

1

Awareness of Thoughts

Student: Is a fantasy the same as "garbage thoughts?"[1] What makes a fantasy, and how do you recognize it as a thought?

Dr. Hora: Who knows the answer to this question? What is a fantasy?

Student: It's a thought in picture form.

Dr. Hora: That's right. That is the correct answer. Yes, it's thinking in pictures.

Student: But don't most thoughts come in the form of pictures?

Dr. Hora: Almost all of them, but it depends on what level you are. Some people think in physical sensations. Have you ever had thoughts not in the form of pictures, but in physical sensations?

Student: Like a "gut feeling."

Dr. Hora: Right.

---

1 - "In the Bible it is described that God said, 'Let there be a firmament—and let it divide the waters…And God made the firmament and divided the waters which were under the firmament from the waters that were above the firmament.' (Genesis 1:6,7). Metapsychiatry interprets this as saying: The waters below the firmament are the 'sea of mental garbage' in which unenlightened man lives and struggles…This is what seems to be going on below the firmament. The firmament itself we understand to be the faculty of awareness, which we call spiritual discernment…Above the firmament is the infinite 'ocean of Love-Intelligence.'" *Beyond the Dream: Awakening to Reality,* Session No. 57, "The Living Soul", p.302.

Student: Fear comes in the form of bodily sensations.

Dr. Hora: Yes. As a matter of fact, the less enlightened we are, the more likely we are to think with our bodies, or with our minds, or with sensations, or symptoms, or even itching. Everything is thoughts. The basic stuff of life is thoughts, and that can come in a variety of forms such as fantasies, emotions, fears, sensations, pain, pleasure, and hate. It's all thoughts. It is helpful to realize that thoughts can express themselves in many ways. It is important to be aware of the thoughts which are happening in consciousness and are being channeled into feelings, emotions, intellectual concepts, physical experiences, and interactional occurrences. All of this is thought.

Everybody has a favorite style of expressing thoughts. Some people prefer to fantasize. Some people prefer to conceptualize. Some people prefer to experience things. This is "style." Everybody has his own style. Now, all this is rather unhealthy, right? It is based on an assumption that we are this physical person who is having these thoughts, who is managing these thoughts, and who is controlling whether the thoughts should be going here or there. As long as the human mind is in control of our lives and experiences, we are sadly unenlightened and we have all kinds of troubles.

The benefit of meditation is that we learn to be aware of our thoughts. Most people don't understand this, and they are not even aware of their thoughts, and that can go on and on and on. Of course, it's very easy to say, "But I am what I am thinking." The French philosopher and mathematician Descartes said, "I think, therefore I am." Of course, he didn't know anything about Metapsychiatry. He was world famous, and because he was very respectable, his pronouncement set back the evolution of spiritual consciousness for years. "I'm thinking, therefore I am." That was his conclusion. Everybody accepted it at face value. It sounds very true, right? I am thinking, therefore I am. In other words, "I am my thoughts." All right. Can this be challenged? If we are not what we are thinking, then what are we? What else is there? What would you say to Descartes today? As students of Metapsychiatry, I challenge you. (*Laughter*) This is very important.

Every time we are in trouble of some kind, we ask the meaning.[2] Do we all know what is meant by "the meaning"?

Student: The mental equivalent of our experience.

Dr. Hora: Yes, a "meaning" is the mental equivalent of our experience. So, we ask, "What is the thought which is expressing itself in this particular problem?" We seek to discern the thought which is manifesting itself as a problem. Therefore, if we would like to be liberated from our problems, we have to recognize that these problems that we are experiencing are certain thoughts. If somebody has a stomach ache, the stomach ache is saying, "I am a thought which produces the stomach ache," right? So, he says, "I think a stomach ache, therefore I am a stomach ache." We are what we think, but interestingly enough, thousands of years before Descartes, the Buddha said, "We are what we think, having become what we have thought." This is not categorically true, but he still didn't give us the answer. If it were true, we would be hopelessly lost. There are millions of people who believe that they are what they think. If somebody thinks he is the King of Spain, he can experience life as the King of Spain. Without enlightenment it is very dangerous and inevitable to be victimized by our own thoughts. Everyone in the world is a victim of his own thoughts, or certain thoughts which

---

2 - "In our pursuit of understanding Reality we have a method based on 'two intelligent questions.' In all our work in Metapsychiatry we ask two questions: (1) What is the meaning of what seems to be? and (2) What is what really is? With the aid of these two questions we are able to separate the real from the seeming, the good from the evil." *Beyond the Dream: Awakening to Reality,* Session No.1, "What is Man?", pg. 11.

were accepted from other people. If somebody says, "You are a jerk," and you accept it, pretty soon you make one mistake after another. It is particularly dangerous if parents tell their child, "You are stupid. You'll never amount to anything, you'll get bad grades, you will be a criminal." All kinds of thoughts are being constantly bestowed on children by their parents. And the children, on high authority, accept it.

Student: What if the parent doesn't say it out loud but thinks, *This child is not as smart as the other child?*

Dr. Hora: It's even worse, because it is a subliminal suggestion which slips deep into the child's heart, into consciousness, and it is believed. We see all kinds of distortions of modes of being in the world which have been subliminally suggested to people. Children in particular are very suggestible; therefore, it is vitally important to understand that we are not what we think, and we are not what anybody else thinks. We deny the validity of the Cartesian claim. Then the question is, "Where do we go from here?" What's the good of disagreeing with such a renowned philosopher?

Student: Metapsychiatry says that we are what God is thinking.

Dr. Hora: Exactly. Now isn't that absurd? Who has ever seen God think? Is God a person who would influence us with His thoughts?

Student: God is infinite Mind, and we are part of it. God does influence us with His thoughts; otherwise we would be in a big jam.

Dr. Hora: Exactly, and anybody who doesn't know it is in a jam all the time.

Student: Is that really the basis of saying that Metapsychiatry, to a large extent, protects us from the ills of the world?

Dr. Hora: Exactly, of course. Is this clear to anybody else? Anybody?

Student: It's understandable, but I think it's hard to always see that because we are so easily distracted. On a day-to-day basis it's not easy to always see God or understand that we are God's thoughts. It's difficult.

Dr. Hora: How could we make it more accessible to know what has been explained?

Student: It is crucial that we distinguish between the thoughts that come to us from God and the garbage thoughts.

Dr. Hora: Exactly. How could we then see our way clearly to be lifted out of the sea of mental garbage into the ocean of Love-Intelligence, where we do not identify ourselves anymore with garbage thoughts? As long as we take the garbage thoughts as reality, we don't even hear the divine ideas, the liberating truths of the Divine Mind. It is very important to understand that we are not made of garbage thoughts, no matter how convincing they are. We are not what we seem to be. We are not what everybody else is telling us that we are. We are not what we would like to be. We are not what we hate to be. We are not what we are convinced that we are. We are not what we can figure out that we are.

In order to come closer to the enlightened way of awareness, first we have to understand that the phenomenological appearance world is not Reality. So, we know what is *not*. We have to first know what isn't, and then we have to seek to find out what *is*. How do we find out what is? For thousands of years, seekers after the Truth tried to find out what is, and most teachers in ancient times said that you must find out what is by the elimination of everything that seems to be. The Zen master said, "If you would like to know who you really are, you have to erase yourself." But you cannot erase yourself, because you get terribly scared. It is a frightening method of seeking enlightenment by trying to say what you are not, which we have done now for about 25 minutes, but you are still here. (*Laughter*)

The great blessing of the teachings of Jesus Christ is that he tells us straight what really is. Yet just because Jesus tells us directly what really is does not help us to see it right away. We either agree with him or we think that it is religious bunk. However, if we begin to consider with radical sincerity that what he is telling us about Reality is true, we begin to see that maybe it *is* true. If we are among those who give him the benefit of the doubt and we start contemplating what he says about what really is, then pretty soon we begin to see little glimmers of light that this is really so. Then we will not become religious preachers who accept a concept of what really is without understanding it. That is a falsehood. You can lie with the Truth. You can accept certain statements and teachings which you have not realized but you agreed with them. Then you use them either to sell yourself a bill of goods or to sell somebody else a bill of goods. You can write books about it and you can teach and you can preach, but you don't really know. You haven't realized it, and you're talking about the Truth, but you are lying, because you make people think that you know, and you don't really know. This is the tragedy of religious preaching and inauthentic intellectuality. Some people get very upset when they hear this. Now, we have authoritative statements by one who really knew. He told us what God is, what Divine Reality is, what Truth is, what really *is*, and we begin to see that maybe it's not the way we thought it was.

Now, the question is, how can we reach a point where we can absolutely see that what Jesus said is so and that we are not just accepting it on faith or believing? Many people think that they should believe what Jesus said or what Hora said. This is a mistake. Believing isn't going to help. Doubting is better than believing, because if you doubt, you are wrestling with the Truth. But if you believe what you accept, you'll never know. You're just a believer. Some religions say that this is all you have to do. You just have to agree and you have to believe, but that's not enough. It doesn't work.

So then, first through meditation we become aware of what isn't, and then through study, prayer, reading, sweating, working, contemplating, confronting, we gradually work ourselves up into a position where things begin to make sense. A new Reality opens up, and we begin to know — here a little, there a little, more and more. It's like when you're sitting at night late, towards the morning, and you begin to see the sunrise. Light, just a little bit of light, and more and more and more, until it's already noon. This is the work that we are engaged in, and the more we see the more there is to see, and then we are no longer our thoughts. We are not this body. We are not what we think. All these things are in the sea of mental garbage. It is a dream of life in the material, illusory world, and then you begin to see you are not part of this world. You are a divine consciousness, an incorporeal spiritual idea in Infinite Mind, and then you become aware that there are thoughts. You are aware of thoughts, but you didn't think these thoughts. They have come to your consciousness spontaneously, always in answer to what is needed. These thoughts are not human thoughts. They are divine thoughts. So, we can say that we are *not* what we think. We are what God is giving us to be aware of. We are the awareness of God's inspired ideas. We are not thinkers anymore. We are recipients of inspired ideas which are flowing more or less freely into consciousness, in accordance to the momentary need.

It's a funny thing, God doesn't speak to us about yesterday and God doesn't speak to us about tomorrow. Jesus said, "Take no thought for tomorrow; sufficient for today is the evil thereof." [3]

3 - "Take therefore no thought for the morrow: for the morrow shall take thought for the things of itself. Sufficient unto the day is the evil thereof." (Matthew 6:34)

In other words, if we are in the habit of thinking in terms of time, time frames, the past, the present, and the future, we are time-bound. God isn't there. God cannot be found in the past, not in the future, and not in the present. In order to be in touch with God, we must be prepared to meet Him in the timelessness of now, from moment to moment. That's the only place you can find God. God is now. God is not yesterday, and God is not tomorrow. God isn't even in the present, but now. "Now is the accepted time. Now is the time of salvation." (2 Corinthians 6:2) The moment we are thinking about yesterday or tomorrow, we're not in touch with God. We're in the sea of mental garbage. This may sound very difficult and far-fetched. How in the world can you just be a divine consciousness which receives a continuous flow of intelligent, valid, needed ideas?

A man was asked, "Where do you live?" He said, "I dwell in the secret place of the Most High."[4] The inquirer said, "Well, yes, but where do you get your mail?" (*Laughter*) So now we say, rightfully, that there are practical considerations. Man has to live in this world even if he is enlightened and not yet ascended out of this world. How do we reconcile this with practical living?

Student: We are in the world but not of it.

Dr. Hora: What would that mean?

Student: We are not humans. We endeavor to see ourselves as transparencies.

Dr. Hora: Yes. And how will that help you to do your banking?

Student: I am aware of God, and God's thoughts couldn't mean garbage thoughts.

---

4 - *See:* Psalm 91

Dr. Hora: The fact is that no matter how enlightened a man is, he still has to be able to function in this world intelligently, effortlessly, efficiently, and effectively. But he has to know that this is just an accommodation, a temporary accommodation to the human-seeming life. He is in this world, but he is not losing touch with God. He is in spiritual consciousness, but he is not losing touch with the necessities of functioning in this world. As a matter of fact, he's functioning with a much greater effectiveness, because he's not distracted by fantasies, by aches and pains, by wants and not-wants, and other things. It would seem that we are living in two realities — in this world but not of it. But if you know that this world is just a temporary appearance world, then you have to accommodate yourself to it; otherwise, you will have to disappear altogether, which is not under your control. Eventually you will be lifted out of this world totally, which is to some people a terrible tragedy of dying, but to other people it is a liberation. It doesn't mean that suicide is a solution to the problem. It's not a solution. Ascension is a solution, but not many people reach that point nowadays. So, we are learning to stay with God, to be receptive to inspired ideas from the Divine Mind, but we don't identify ourselves anymore as physical bodies, as physical persons, as intellects, or as emotional baggage of some kind. All this is losing its importance. We see it, we know it, we understand it, but it's not really important.

If an unenlightened individual gets a pain in his pinky, everything else disappears, and all he is conscious of is that little pain in the pinky. He makes a federal case out of pleasure, pain, physical experience, every sensation, and relationship problems. All these things. The enlightened individual takes notice of it, but it's not important.

Reality was revealed to us by the great teacher of mankind, and all that is required is to understand it.

Student: What do you mean by "temporary accommodation?"

Dr. Hora: Well, temporary means that it's not forever. You put up with it and don't *kvetch* [complain] about it.

Student: You're saying that "being in the world" is a temporary accommodation. What are we accommodating?

Dr. Hora: Whatever is going on. Whatever has to be done. You go grocery shopping no matter how enlightened you are. (*Laughter*) You go to the grocery store. You do the shopping but don't overbuy. Right? (*Laughter*) Some people just buy too much.

Student: I would like to ask a question about "Yes is good, but no is also good." [5] Certainly, in the context of looking at outcomes, you say that something might occur and it would be good, but if it doesn't occur, that is also good, thus letting God's ideas unfold. But I sometimes get confused, because there are certain things that we actually see as *not* good. Sin is not good. Death is not good. I'm confused, because it isn't about saying that things that aren't ofGod can be thought of as good.

Dr. Hora: Well, the principle lacks three words. Perhaps it would have been better to write "Yes is good, but no is also good *under Divine control.*" When God is in control, and we're aware of God being in control of the situation, then yes is good, but no is also good. From a human standpoint, of course, we want things to be pleasurable and not painful. We have made up our minds what should be and what shouldn't be. But the principles of Metapsychiatry refer to a consciousness which is aware of Divine Mind's control.

Student: Does this relate to karmic law, where we have to suffer from our ignorance in order to learn?

---

5 - The Fourth Principle of Metapsychiatry.

Dr. Hora: That is not karmic law. Karmic law says, "As you sow, so shall you reap." Whether you learn or you don't learn, it's going on and on. If we have a problem, we find the meaning, we correct our thoughts, then we are learning and we are making progress.

Problems are lessons designed for our edification.[6] For instance, we might be in a situation in which we have theater tickets, andwe think, *Tonight we have to go to the theater. We have the tickets.We want to go to the theater, and we think that is what should be.* How many people would say "Well, if we can go to the theater it'sall right, but if we cannot go it's also all right?" An enlightened individual could say that, and he wouldn't kill himself trying to get to the theater; whereas an unenlightened individual would most likely get there uncomfortably and with stress. We have to allow that maybe something good could come out of not getting what we want. Very often it is so. At such times people could say, "Yes is good, but no is even better." Maybe it was a lousy show. (*Laughter*) Maybe there was some trouble — somebody yelled "Fire!" This principle helps us not to insist on having our way. We're not so uptight.

Student: You told me a story once. You were going into town to buy something, and as you were looking for a parking space, you just got an idea that it would be better to go home. And when you went home, you received a very important call. It was important for you to be there to respond to that call. If you had had a mindset about doing what you set out to do, you would not have been able to be helpful to that caller.

Dr. Hora: That's a very good example, even though I must have lied. (*Laughter*) That's a joke. Is it all right to lie for didactic purposes? No, it's not right, because it shakes the confidence of the students. It must have happened but I don't remember. (*Laughter*)

---

6 - The Eighth Principle of Metapsychiatry.

Student: I remember him telling that story too.

Dr. Hora: An additional witness. (*Laughter*)

Student: It seems that things have a way of turning out for the better, even though at the time it's not what we wanted. If you wait a little while, it seems like it's better that it worked out that way.

Dr. Hora: It helps to keep the principle in mind. If you don't keep this in mind, you become willful, bitter, and upset. All kinds of invalid thoughts will flood your consciousness and it is not going to be better. But this principle gives you a degree of humility, and it is humility that attracts the good in life. Willfulness attracts negative experiences, but humility makes everything smoother and more harmonious and positive, because humility is a spiritual quality. So, the principle has validity beyond its logical interpretation. It has an existential impact when we do not insist on having it our way. "Hold the pickle, hold the lettuce, have it *your* way."[7] Right? (*Laughter*)

Student: So those examples that were given validate that principle.

Dr. Hora: Yes. Sure.

Student: If we accept something that is said here, without fully realizing or understanding it, and then it's validated—

Dr. Hora: Then you begin to understand little by little, and we speak about a "demonstration." What is a "demonstration?" When a Truth which we know about validates itself in our experience, we understand, *Aha! Surely this is so.* When we realize it. When Reality becomes real to us, we have a realization. A total realization comes from hundreds and thousands of little "Aha's."

---

7 - Commercial jingle written for Burger King restaurants by Barry Manilow, 1971.

Student: You mentioned earlier that thoughts can be more damaging when they are nonverbal. How can we become more aware of these nonverbal thoughts?

Dr. Hora: Good question. The more we practice observing our thoughts under all circumstances, when we're alone, when we are with others, during the day, at night, even when we are on the subway, we must always be able to observe our thoughts. If you do this you become proficient in it. It is a secret ability which you have. You develop an ability to observe your thoughts. Then you will become aware of the subliminal suggestions which you have absorbed any time during your lifetime or even today.

I heard that in some department stores they are using subliminal suggestions such as, "don't steal," or "buy this." You're not aware of it. It's set up in music recordings that the management plays over the public address system. You can walk through the store and get an irresistible urge to buy something that you don't need at all. And you buy it! This is going on everywhere. Even before electronics were invented, parents knew how to give such suggestions to their children — "Love your mother!" Yes? (*Laughter*) There are all kinds of things. We're exposed to these things, and if we are not trained in awareness, it works in us. Sometimes we are startled by having done something which we wouldn't otherwise do.

Student: The difficulty that I see is when there's a pleasant experience, I'm not as vigilant. And that seems to be the most dangerous.

Dr. Hora: Yes, sure. There are various situations when we drop our guard. We can also be hypnotized into various things like being sick. Sickness in someone can be very suggestive, so we think we should feel the same. We have spoken about the problem of empathy and sympathy.[8] If you're in the habit of sympathizing with

8 - See: *Beyond the Dream: Awakening to Reality.* Session No. 53, "Compassion", p. 282.

people, or empathizing, you're going to feel it. And you think, *I'm a nice person, because I can feel what somebody else is feeling.* It makes you feel like a nice person, but it also makes you a recipient of the problem without realizing it. You get the problem. You just pick it up. You watch television, and there are attractive ways of suggesting you should be sick. It is very suggestive. I am sure thousands of people get sick every night from watching television, because those commercials are scientifically designed to have an impact on us. The result is you rush out to buy the medicine that was recommended. We are constantly subjected to these kinds of influences. The protection is: be alert, be aware, and refuse.

2

Joy

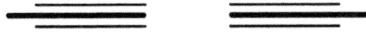

Student: What is the meaning of being happy to see someone who hasn't been here in a while? It's a good feeling.

Dr. Hora: It's called "love." Enter into the joy of the Lord, and try to stay there. (*Laughter*)

A Zen Master spoke of how enlightened individuals recognize each other instantly when they meet. How is that possible? It's like one thief knowing another. (*Laughter*) If we know that God is Joy and Love and Intelligence and that everyone is here for God, then joy is spontaneous. When we meet each other, it's spontaneous joy. It just comes out. It's not pretending. It's not dreaming. It's a joy in seeing a transparency for God. We know everyone is a transparency for God. Even if they don't know it, we know it, right? Especially students of Metapsychiatry who are constantly reminded of this. (*Laughter*)

To be joyous is very important. A joyless life is not worth living. Without joy life is nothing, absolutely nothing. Unfortunately, we see many people who don't even realize that they are joyless, and that is very sad.

Student: Is that what depression is?

Dr. Hora: Yes. Joylessness. When we are depressed, we don't know that there is a God. All we know is we don't feel so good. We are here for ourselves; but when we are here for God, we lose sight of ourselves. Joy is spontaneous and always present.

Student: Is that why children seem naturally joyous?

Dr. Hora: Exactly.

Student: But then I see day after day in school how it is knocked out of them. It's disturbing.

Dr. Hora: That's right, unfortunately. People who don't know who they are, are very often joyless.

Student: Often students are discouraged by certain teachers.

Dr. Hora: Oh yes, sure. Jesus said, "My joy I leave unto you; my joy no man taketh from thee."[1] It is interesting that we lose our sense of joy if we get involved in interpersonal relationships. We lose it. We rob one another of joy. Isn't that fantastic? How does that happen?

Student: Is it rivalry, jealousy—things like that? Maybe a wife sees her husband having a good time and she's not, and she gets competitive. That could rob him of joy.

Dr. Hora: Yes. Oh, yes. Joy is the normal way to be. This sounds strange because there is so little evidence of it.

Student: I spent a few hours today helping a young woman. When I arrived at her home I was feeling fine, happy, joyous; however, she

---

1 - "These things have I spoken unto you, that my joy might remain in you, and that your joy might be full." (John 15:11) "I will see you again, and your heart shall rejoice, and your joy no man taketh from you." (John 16:22)

was miserable. Somebody crossed the street with her child, and she said, "That makes me so nervous when she crosses that way." And I thought that it is not any of her business, but I didn't say it. Throughout the day she had a hostility to things that had nothing to do with her. I started to sink. I could see the invalid thoughts, but it was hard to protect myself. The hostility, the anger, and minding everybody else's business seemed contagious.

Dr. Hora: Yes. Joy is a treasure and we must not let anyone rob us of it.

Student: What is the meaning of it being easy for us to lose? Is it that we don't have a full appreciation of it, or that we are not always fully aware? In this particular example was this student somehow getting involved with the young woman's view?

Dr. Hora: How many people know who they really are?

Student: We have a hard enough time. (*Laughter*)

Dr. Hora: Yes. This is a best kept secret. People don't know who they are.

Student: How can they know? How can we know?

Dr. Hora: You are being told here every week. (*Laughter*)

Student: We have a chance to know, but the average person has no way of knowing. If we understand that they have no way of knowing, this is compassion.

Dr. Hora: Yes. Certainly.

Student: Our protection, so that we don't lose our joy, is that if we really know who we are, we wouldn't be mesmerized, or hypnotized, or critical, or fearful because we would have assurance.

Dr. Hora: There is a Christmas song which says, "Joy to the world, the Lord is come."[2] Now, what does that mean? People are singing it. Does that have any meaning? We can say that "the Lord" refers to the Christ. So, Christ has come, so what? If you think that Christ was a person, it makes no sense, right? So what else is it? The whole world should be joyous because the Christ has come. What is this Christ?

Student: Consciousness?

Dr. Hora: The Christ reveals to us our true identity. We are Christ. We are not joyless, unhappy, fearful, angry, jealous persons. Jesus was a transparency through whom the Christ was revealed to the world and he knew it. He was a man who was naturally joyous, and he knew that this was also everyone's identity. So, if we understand the meaning of the Christ, we will be joyous, because he said we are also that. What he revealed to the world, that is what we also are. So, right understanding of our identities is the secret of joy. Unprecarious joy. If you know that you are nothing, you cannot take yourself seriously, right? If you cannot take yourself seriously, you must be joyous. If, however, you have the erroneous self-concept of being a person who has possessions and who has a job and who is doing things, and who worries what other people should or should not be thinking, then you take yourself seriously, and there is no joy. There is no joy.
What is a relationship?

Student: A joy killer. (*Laughter*)

Dr. Hora: That's right. That's very true. How do relationships kill the joy?

---

2 - "Joy to the World", by Isaac Watts, 1719.

Student: The "four horsemen."[3]

Dr. Hora: Could you explain?

Student: Well, envy, comparison thinking, vicious, malicious, unloving thoughts. Even if it is under the guise of friendliness.

Dr. Hora: Yes. So, what does the world suffer from? The world suffers from relationships. Very simple. Jesus said, "When two or three are gathered in my name I shall be among them."[4] What does that mean?

Student: If two or three people get together who are like-minded in the search for Christ, then Christ is there.

Dr. Hora: Right, yes, and do they have relationships? In the presence of Christ there are no relationships. What is there?

Student: Joint participation.

Dr. Hora: Jean-Paul Sartre wrote a play, *No Exit*. He put three people in a hotel room, and these three people couldn't get out of this hotel room. They had no radio or stereo or television. What were they doing? They were constantly involved with their relationships with each other. Then he says, "This is hell." This is the conclusion of the play: hell is people. When people are together and they are unenlightened, they are constantly engaged in relationships with each other. There is no joy there. There is suffering. There is all kinds of suffering.

---

3 - "The Four Horsemen are: Envy, Jealousy, Rivalry, and Malice." *Beyond the Dream: Awakening to Reality*, Session 56: "How Mature is God?", p. 297.

4 - "For where two or three are gathered together in my name, there am I in the midst of them." (Matthew 18:20)

Student: The state of being together when Christ is among us, that is not the opposite of relationship; but that's the way to be with others. Is that correct?

Dr. Hora: Now what would be the opposite of relationships?

Student: Anger.

Dr. Hora: Anger is a relationship.

Student: Isolation.

Dr. Hora: Isn't isolation a relationship?

Student: Didn't you say the opposite?

Dr. Hora: Yes, you are right; that's right. It would seem to be separateness and isolation. Yes. Let's face it, isolation is also a relationship. How could people be together without having relationships?

Student: Wouldn't it be joint participation in the good of God?

Dr, Hora: What would that be?

Student: The qualities of their values.

Dr. Hora: What kind of values would that be?

Student: Spiritual values.

Dr. Hora: What's that?

Student: In the past, you used the analogies of a tree and the Sun. The leaves on the tree are each independent, and so are the rays of the Sun. They don't have relationships with each other.

Dr. Hora: And the leaves of the tree are sustained by the tree.

Student: Also, the waves of the ocean.

Dr. Hora: Right. Yes. There would be harmonious coexistence and there would be joy and peace and funny jokes. Lots of laughter and no sicknesses. Would you believe that if people knew how to live without interaction, they would never get sick and they might live to be 150 years? Today it is not considered an impossibility, but one would have to know how to be in this world without interaction.

Now if you consider your day, every day, how much time passes in one day where there is no interaction? It is perhaps just minutes – on the best day. (Laughter) Otherwise, mentally we're forever involved with interaction. The only escape would be ceaseless prayer. What would that mean? It is a great protection against interaction thinking. What is ceaseless prayer? If you want to have a long life and you never want to be sick, you have to practice ceaseless prayer. The Bible speaks about it, right? This is from the Bible: ceaseless prayer. [5]

Student: Mindfulness?

Dr. Hora: Mindfulness of what?

Student: Mindfulness of Infinite Mind.

Dr. Hora: That's very good, but is there more?

Student: Mostly monitoring of your thoughts ceaselessly. Constantly see where you are at.

Dr. Hora: Where do you have to be at?

5 - "Pray without ceasing." (Thessalonians 5:17)

Student: Watch your thoughts.

Dr. Hora: If we watch our thoughts, we will find that we are thinking about what others are thinking about what we are thinking — right? In other words, ceaseless prayer means constant conscious attention to be aware of the Truth of our Being. Reminding ourselves who we are, what we are, where we are, and what our purpose is in life. Can you sustain that? It is not easy, but it's worth trying, or putting in the effort, because eventually you will find that more and more time elapses without your having any interaction thoughts. For instance, if you are a musician and if you are singing or playing an instrument and you're good at it, and you're not just a thinker, but a *real* musician, and you are immersed in the music rather than in what people think about your performance, you will find that music will set you free of people. The music will become a form of prayer which is protecting you from interaction thoughts. This is the secret of the longevity of many musicians. They are in a dimension of consciousness where interaction thoughts do not intrude while they are immersed in the music. Perhaps a good connoisseur of music will also have these benefits. Music is very healthy if you know how to listen with a whole heart. Because it protects us from interaction thoughts; it has a healing effect on people. So, the right kind of attention to music is very good. But the essential issue for the human condition is how to escape interaction thinking.

Student: Is there such a thing as interdependency, like at work, where one person does this job and another does that job?

Dr. Hora: Sure. It's called the *folie à deux*. What is *folie à deux*? People think about each other and influence each other and pressure each other and seduce each other and provoke each other. It is the normal way to live in an office or in the family or anywhere. Interaction is the normal human condition which people are immersed in. And they pay a terrible price — a terrible price. We also know the breakdowns in individuals occur in close-knit families and in corporate workplaces more often than anywhere else in the world. People literally destroy each other. The closer they are to each other, the more destructive they are towards each other, and eventually they can die from it. It's because of the frictions and the rivalries and the jealousies that people experience in this kind of setting without knowing how to protect themselves. And the Bible says, "Because thou hast made the Lord thy habitation, there shall no evil befall thee, neither shall any plague come nigh thy dwelling." (Psalm 91) How many people understand this message? It is a mental hygiene message. How can you preserve your health, your sanity, your peace, your freedom? Only if God is the first priority in your thoughts. Then you are protected from interaction thinking.

There is a movement in the United States called the "survivalist movement." Do you know about the survivalists? These are people who are forever preparing for disaster and practicing to protect themselves from other people who might come too close. They see a threat from relationships, so they practice in the wild with guns and store up food so they won't have to come in contact withpeople. These are survivalists. We are also learning how to survivein a civilized world. It isn't easy. Psychology says that the measureof your mental health is the number of relationships that you are able to be engaged in. Did you know that?

Student: It's also a sign of trust, for you to trust other people.

Dr. Hora: Oh yes, that's wonderful, (*Laughing*) trusting other people.

Student: To really trust—trying to develop good relationships and trust.

Dr. Hora: Yes, all right, sure. A teenager might steal something or get into trouble, and their parents ask them, "Did you do that?"

And they say, "What's the matter, don't you trust me?" You're supposed to trust your family members, and if something is wrong they'll say "It's because you didn't trust me. It's your fault!" You are supposed to trust people. It's absolute nonsense. We neither trust anybody nor do we mistrust anybody. The issue of trusting is a non-issue. What is the issue?

Student: Being here for God.

Dr. Hora: Is that the issue? That is a cliché, a Metapsychiatric cliché. The issue is seeing. People have to see what is going on, and if you cannot see, then trusting doesn't help and mistrusting doesn't help. You either see or you don't see.

Student: What is it you see?

Dr. Hora: Motivation. Interests. We have to see where people are. "What's the matter? Don't you trust me?" (*Laughter*) How many times have you heard that, yes? The assumption is that you are supposed to trust me.

Student: There are certain individuals I'm with a great deal, and I find it difficult not to have expectations of them and to let them be. You have often told me to keep my mouth shut.

Dr. Hora: Not very successfully. (*Laughter*)

Student: But it seems to me I so often want to protect them, though it's none of my business. So what am I supposed to do? I don't want to see them get hurt. They don't know any better. They mean well. So how do I learn to shut my mouth, because you keep telling me there's no relationship. But if I see it, what do I do with it?

Dr. Hora: It reminds me of a story two weeks ago. Somebody told me that her husband spilled some water on the beautiful new floor in the kitchen, and she said, "I hope you will wipe it up." Whereupon he exploded and said, "No!" He refused to wipe it up. (*Laughing*) She wanted to help him to do the right thing, and of course because she told him to, he wouldn't do it. Fortunately, she had to leave. Later she was told that you cannot tell people what they should do. Indeed, when she gave up the thought that he should clean up the kitchen floor, she came home and it was very neat and clean. He did it by himself. You don't have to tell people anything. Not because you trust them, but because you trust God. They are here for God whether they know it or not. We don't trust people, but we have to behold them in the context of God, and then we can let them be and they usually do the right thing. We are not agonizing over them, and trying to trust them or not trust them, or trying to pretend that we are trusting them or checking up on whether they really do something or not.

Student: Is it relevant, though, in this case to ask the meaning of him spilling the water on the floor?

Dr. Hora: That would be entering into somebody's consciousness without authorization. You have to knock first. (*Laughter*) We don't speculate about the meanings of people's experiences if they are not asking for it.

Student: So, you see it happening and you just let it be?

Dr. Hora: Yes. You could pray, acknowledging that this individual is also a transparency for God and is here for God. You are not anybody's keeper. We are not each other's keepers. God is everyone's keeper.

Student: To me it wouldn't be so much that I am his keeper, but that I'm thinking how this is impacting me.

Dr. Hora: Who else? (*Laughter*)

Student: So, I'm taking it personally?

Dr. Hora: You bet. (*Laughter*)

Student: Then I scream.

Dr. Hora: Right. Right.

Student: I could have responded by wiping it up immediately and not saying anything. Is that invalid?

Dr. Hora: No. That's okay. You can do that. But it is what you are thinking that is important.

Student: If I thought the water was spilled deliberately, that's one thing. But what if I just saw water being spilled and wiped it up anddidn't think about it.

Dr. Hora: But you could be thinking what a nice person you are.

Student: Oh, that's probably what I would be thinking. (*Laughter*) I'm always trying to be nice. It seems like it is automatic.

Dr. Hora: Nice persons get into trouble. It's not nice to be nice.

Student: So, if we do see something and we interfere, we are also saying, "I know better than you."

Dr. Hora: Sure. If you are the keeper of another person, then he is your slave and you are superior to him. You cannot be the keeper of anybody. But you can say, as Jesus said, "I am among you ashe that serves." (Luke 22:27) What did he mean? Do we have to become servants of our fellow man, so that we would thereby become religious heroes?

Student: We serve others by being beneficial.

Dr. Hora: No. A beneficial presence doesn't serve anybody.

Student: Because there's nobody there.

Dr. Hora: No, because he is a servant of God. He wipes off the floor because God is order. Not because he is a nice person. Not because the other is a jerk (*Laughter*) but because God is order, and a transparency expresses the orderliness of God. And there's no interaction in the thoughts, whatsoever.

Student: So everything is for God's sake.

Dr. Hora: Who else? There is nobody else.

Student: A long time ago we talked about taking out the garbage. You said if that is what is needed, you just take it out, and there is no "You should do it" or "I should do it." Is that the same thing?

Dr. Hora: Yes, it is the same thing. "I am among you as one that serveth." We serve God not for religious reasons, but because we are transparencies for God. All our thoughts and actions and attitudes manifest the qualities of God, which are joy, love, intelligence, beauty, harmony, freedom, etc. Right? And that's the secret of survival. For marriages, too. When a marriage deteriorates, it's a "relationship." Then you have all kinds of complications, and of course the prevalent view of marriage is that it's a "marital relationship."

Student: Regarding "joy," I still have a problem with this. I know it's not a feeling, but it so closely approximates happiness.

Dr. Hora: It *is* happiness.

Student: It seems to be a state of feeling happy and joyful, and yet you always tell us that joy is not a feeling. How would you cultivate joy?

Dr. Hora: You cultivate joy through ceaseless prayer. "Enter into the joy of thy Lord." (Matthew 25: 21, 23) Ceaseless prayer is a constant, conscious acknowledgement of the truth of our being, and the effect of this sincere prayer is joy. We become joyous, which is synonymous with happiness. There's no other happiness. What people call happiness can be all kinds of things. Somebody you don't like drops dead, you can be happy. (*Laughter*) There aremany ways that people find what they call "happiness," but it's just pleasure and feeling good or something like that.

Student: How do you recognize the difference between "joy" and "feeling good?"

Dr. Hora: Feelings are organismic experiences. Joy is a quality of consciousness. It is not in your body. It is not an experience. It is an awareness. True happiness is quiet joy.

Student: It seems to me that I am filled with gratitude at those times.

Dr. Hora: Not just for you, but for everyone. Gratitude is the door to joy. That's what Metapsychiatry claims. It's a door to joy. Enter into the joy of the Lord. It's a visible door. There's a sign on it: "Gratitude." (*Laughter*)

Student: Most people, I think, find it hard to be grateful.

Dr. Hora: Yes, that's true. What's your point?

Student: I have a problem with thinking *I'll be grateful when...*, like when a certain condition is met. Perhaps enlightenment, perhaps if a certain circumstance were met in the future.

Dr. Hora: Yes. In the future. The future is fear, the past is pain, the present is vanity, but God is now. Now is the accepted time. Now is the time of salvation and true happiness.[6] Most people live in a consciousness of time, either in the past or in the future or in the present. Enlightenment is timeless. Enlightened individuals live in the infinitude of timelessness. Now. Every moment is now, and that's where God can be realized. God cannot be found in any time frame. You cannot put God into a frame. God is not in the past and God is not in the future and God is not in the present. It's a little mind-boggling when you consider it, but God is now, from moment to moment now. That's Reality. Time frames are concepts. There's really no such thing as "time." It's a practical, useful human concept. It makes civilized functioning possible. You might think that if you live in the timeless, you would not be very practical, but that's not true. It's possible to function very well in time frames even though we know that they are just helpful accommodations for practical functioning in the human condition. But God doesn't take notice of time. There is no time in Divine Reality. There is also no space in Divine Reality. No matter how many people are in this room, there's no space problem, right? There's only one problem — interaction thinking, when people look at each other and think, *I wonder what they are thinking about what I am thinking.*

Student: What is the meaning of being a slave to time?

Dr. Hora: Well, that would be considered an erroneous idea. There are people who are very much troubled by time. They can never make the train on time; they're always late. There are some who

---

6 - "For he saith, I have heard thee in a time accepted, and in the day of salvation have I succoured thee: behold, now is the accepted time; behold, now is the day of salvation." (2 Corinthians 6:2)

are always too early. As a famous psychoanalyst said, "If you are early, you're anxious. If you're late, you are resisting. If you're on time, you are compulsive." (*Laughter*) But if you are enlightened, you never show up here. (*Laughter*)

3

Spiritual Values

Student: A few months ago we were talking about "it is good to be good," and I have been working with that idea. Are we talking about good thoughts?

Dr. Hora: Well, what do we mean by "good?"

Student: I guess "Godly" in some sense.

Dr. Hora: Godly? Godliness is good, but good is not necessarily Godly good. Just as love is very seldom Love. It can be all kinds of things, but what is *real* good? It is an interest in benevolence. It is rejoicing in the good of another. Have you ever been aware that it makes you happy to see somebody else prosper? What do you think?

Student: It is very easy to be envious.

Dr. Hora: It is. And it is very easy to be insincere and manipulative. But *real* good is not only unselfish, it is selfless. It derives happiness from seeing something that is beneficial to whomever; whether we are involved personally or not, we rejoice in the good of another. Now, what business is it of yours or ours if somebody is having a good experience?

Student: It indicates the presence of God.

Dr. Hora: That's right. Exactly. The good of another can be a proof, a demonstration, a reminder that there is such a thing as genuine good—nonpersonal, nonconditional good. And that is the *real* good.

Student: Then, Dr. Hora, are we "being good" when we see that good and rejoice in that good?

Dr. Hora: No, we are not being good, we are being enlightened, because "good" is a value judgment, right? Too many sincere Christians and religionists make an effort to be good and generous. They give food, various things, and money to help others. That is *behavior* and you can never tell if it is genuine or just pretense. But being good in a genuine way is not a value judgment. It is an "aha." It is a discernment of God's presence and action in the world. Ordinarily we see just evil in the world. Everything seems evil. We see that very often; but when we understand that *it is good to be good*, it means that we realize we have the opportunity to see God's hand in the affairs of man—women too. (*Laughing*) That's enlightenment.

Student: When you speak about "it is good to be good" as part of "the love of being loving," then it seems that spiritual qualities might be expressed just for their own sake. We say, "the joy of being joyful," but it is difficult, because I think it is hard to rise above the object-oriented world, to see it happening in consciousness, or manifesting itself in objects. It seems to take a leap of understanding, because if we are joyful, it is generally because something happened.

Dr. Hora: We are learning to be aware of an objectless universe. Do you understand that?

Student: Yes, because we can maybe think about it this way: that we are paying more attention to ideas in consciousness than to a tangible reality. Like, for example, I might hurt myself or something; I could focus on that, but that doesn't help. It helps more to be aware of the thoughts.

Dr. Hora: Absolutely.

Student: It's an idea rather than a physical something.

Dr. Hora: What is the object in an objectless universe? What do you think?

Student: I don't know. That seems like a koan.

Dr. Hora: You wouldn't touch it with a ten-foot pole. *(Laughing)* It is very simple. No?

Student: Seeing the object you see—or understand...

Dr. Hora: Being aware of the Divine Reality as All in all. Immortal Mind governs the universe. Have you ever seen Immortal Mind?

Student: You can see it at work, like you can see the wind at work, but you can't see the wind.

Dr. Hora: Right. The wind bloweth where it listeth, and where it goeth and cometh— *(pausing)*— no man knoweth.[1] *(Laughter)*

Student: Doesn't enlightenment mean seeing the Divine manifesting? You don't have direct vision of the Divine itself?

Dr. Hora: Well, you see Reality. Reality is non-dimensional; therefore, goodness is not a person or a state of mind. It is a quality of consciousness, and the more enlightened we are the more we see

---

1 -"The wind bloweth where it listeth, and thou hearest the sound thereof, but canst not tell whence it cometh, and whither it goeth...." (John 3:8)

the non-dimensional, objectless Reality, and that's God. This is very difficult for us, because we are conditioned from childhood on to see time and space and interaction and three-dimensional objects in the world or in the universe. Everything is objectified. People are billiard balls crashing against each other. And we can see the good concretely experienced by someone.

Student: So would it be an objectifying thing to ask for an example?

Dr. Hora: I just gave you several examples. Ancient philosophers ask the question, *"Cui bono?"* "Good for whom?" Isn't that the normal way you talk about good? You ask, "For whom?" If you are on the path to enlightenment, you don't ask, "For whom?" You ask, "What?" because what blesses one blesses the other also. So, we don't have to be concerned about for whom the good is good. It doesn't matter. The good is manifesting itself as the presence of God, and it is infinite, non-objective. We have heard a lot about non-objective art, haven't we? It is not so prevalent among us anymore, but at one time great artists were struggling to produce works of art which were impossible to objectify. There was an artist who was dripping and pouring paint. What was his name?

Student: "Objectless expressionism." Jackson Pollock.

Dr. Hora: Jackson Pollock. Yes, he and others liked to produce non-objective works of art, in sculpture, in painting, and there was a guy who tried to do it in music. Do you remember John Cage? He would sit down at the piano and not play. *(Laughing)* I do this all the time. *(Laughing)* He became famous. Anyway, you cannot produce non-dimensional images in a two- or three-dimensional medium, but you can hint in that direction. You can hint at it.

Student: Is it valid, though, when you think about it, that there seems to be a quest in mankind for beauty in art forms? People try to create love, it seems to me, in mankind. We believe we have to create it.

Dr. Hora: Some works of art which express beauty are called "kitsch" by some. Are you familiar with that? It is being spurned by some, which is very childish and immature, because it is often just expressing beautiful objects, such as flowers and landscapes. This is not appreciated by "serious" artists. I think in our modern world, art has often distanced itself from beauty and harmony in attempting to make statements about "reality." The issue in modern art is "reality" rather than beauty. You see ugliness in art galleries—lots of ugliness. But the artist was not interested in beauty, because that is seen as very naïve. Grandma Moses was interested in beauty. So, there is another value here, portrayal of Reality, which is an impossibility because Reality is non-dimensional. But you can express harmony. We have a painting in the basement at our home in Bedford. Mrs. Hora was preparing a canvas for a picture which she had planned to paint, and this painting consists of three parts of different colors. There is nothing there. It's just a prepared canvas, and whoever goes down to the basement is startled by this "modern" painting. "How beautiful, and how artistic it is!" *(Laughter)*

It reminds me of when a dignitary from another culture, maybe China, visited a concert in New York. It was a big, elegant, musical event, and after the concert he was asked what he thought of it. He said that the best part was in the beginning when they were tuning up the orchestra. *(Laughing) That* he could appreciate. The rest was just organized noise. *(Laughter)*

Student: I was just thinking: you said things like, "It is good to be good. It is joyful to be joyous," and I know it is invalid, but I keep thinking, *What's in it for me? (Laughter)*

Dr. Hora: Cui bono?

Student: What makes the difference that somebody could genuinely love being loving, or say, "It is good to be good," and sincerely mean it without any concern for *what's in it for me?* What makes that possible?

Dr. Hora: Now imagine that you are looking at a beautiful sunset, right? What's in it for you? Why even consider it? What would you say?

Student: It is hard to think of anything.

Student: Dr. Hora, I understand that because it's in nature, but when watching the TV show *Lifestyles of the Rich and Famous*, it seems personal. There is probably envy going on. I'm thinking, *Wow! I'd like to have that!*

Dr. Hora: Money and a yacht?

Student: It seems as if people have possessions. Maybe that's what it is. It seems to be a personal possession or a physical characteristic or something. Somehow it seems harder spiritually to overcome. It's hard to appreciate it for what it is, that it is coming from God, rather than thinking, *They have it and I don't.*

Dr. Hora: That reminds me of a story about a Zen monk who lived a very solitary life somewhere in the woods, and one day a robber came to him and attacked him and said, "Give me everything that you have or I will kill you." So, this Zen monk started to laugh and said, "I only have this shirt which I am wearing." He said, "Give me that shirt off your back." So, the monk gave him the shirt and kept laughing, and the thief said, "What are you laughing about? You have nothing. What do you have to laugh about?" The monk said, "I wish I could give you my real treasure." "What's that?" asked the robber. The monk said, "You look at the moon, but you don't appreciate the beauty of it. That is my real treasure. The ability to appreciate the beauty of the moon. It is not a possession. You cannot buy it. You cannot sell it. But it can make you happy, if you can appreciate it." That story is sort of a *mondo*[2] to educate certain people who contemplate real values in life. Real values are not

---

2 - Mondos are collected stories told by Zen teachers.

material possessions, but faculties which enable us to appreciate the beauty of God, or the good of God. You cannot touch it, nobody made it, you can't get an award for it, right? You cannot brag about it, but it can elevate your consciousness into beholding the good of God. That's real art—the non-objective, non-dimensional, non-material quality of God.

There are people who travel throughout the world, because they know the value of art. There is a history of rich Americans traveling to France, to Paris, and buying up Impressionist and Post-Impressionist paintings. People thought, *What is this with Americans?* Were they suddenly so spiritually enlightened that they can appreciate the value of these paintings? People from other cultures and nations had no idea and could not understand why these Americans spent money on what was seen by many as trash. They went to Montmartre and other famous places. They bought it up, they brought it home, and they exhibited it, and then they put it in vaults. *(Laughter)* What does that indicate? The values which they had were not as sincere connoisseurs with aesthetic appreciation. They were primarily attracted by the prospects of the monetary value on the art market. It was a wonderful investment. It brought millions of dollars, in the vaults, and then when they needed money they could sell it and make a tremendous profit. Who knows how many masterpieces there are in private vaults which people have accumulated? Even the Nazis did it. Mass murderer Hermann Göering was a most avaricious, acquisitive man. He sent out his emissaries, high-ranking Nazi military men, to requisition works of art wherever they could find them, and they would bring them to him. If your appreciation is in the direction of commercial value, you don't really see the beauty of these works of art, you see the dollar bills which they represent. It is a very refined, subtle issue. Many collectors are mostly unaware of the aesthetic value. For someone who is aware of the aesthetic value, it doesn't matter if the value doesn't increase in the market, but it makes his soul glad.

Now, what could be more important than this joy of awareness of true values—spiritual beauty and creativity? There are different ways of looking, and seeing, and appreciating, but if we learn here that, "It is good to be good," we don't mean the collecting of objects. It is completely non-dimensional, non-objective, spiritual goodness. You don't get nothin' in return. *(Laughter)*

Student: So, it is not "experiences" either?

Dr. Hora: No.

Student: I mean you are not rejoicing in somebody's good experience.

Dr. Hora: Well, that's permitted.

Student: Yes, but you are talking about something beyond that.

Dr. Hora: We can rejoice in the good of another, because when we see the good of another we see that there is such a thing as goodness. So, it is all right. It is not selfish and it's not unselfish.
It is selfless. It is enlightened. We had a session not long ago on discerning the difference between "selfish," "unselfish," and "selfless."[3] (Turning to a student) So, you were meditating on, "It is good to be good?"

Student: Yes.

Dr. Hora: One of our friends in the group had a private session, and she was getting a coughing spell, and she got panicky because she couldn't stop coughing. I was inspired to say to her, "Listen, it is good to be good," and the coughing spell stopped just like that. She asked, "How is this? What does it mean that now I can breathe and the panic disappeared, just because you said, 'It is good to be good?'" What happened in that session? Ever since then she hasn't

3 - See : Chapter 7 : "Selflessness" in *Encounters with Wisdom, Book Three.*

been coughing anymore. Some students have heard about this and tried to apply it like a formula to their problems, but they have not found it helpful. I was inspired at that moment because I could see that while we were talking she was very envious of somebody, and this envy had malicious thoughts with it. So, when I said, "It's good to be good," this completely demolished the whole structure of her thoughts. She had been panicky at not being able to stop coughing.

Student: Is that the same as when we replace an invalid idea with a valid one? If we are involved with envy, for example, or we're angry or something, when we say, "It is good to be good," then we are orienting towards reality. There is goodness. There is good.

Dr. Hora: Yes. Her mentality was towards malicious envy, and when she heard this, in effect it destroyed the structure. There is a structure to our thought, and the perspective for her was destroyed by this simple statement. Ever since then she keeps asking, "What do you mean?" She still cannot explain it, but it stops her from coughing. Sometimes God whispers in your ear just the right words which can heal somebody's problem. Somebody could say, "Well, you must have read these words in some book." No. It's not in the Bible. It's not in philosophy. Nobody told me this. It just made sense in that particular moment, and it had this healing effect.

Student: Is it important to understand how that works?

Dr. Hora: How it works?

Student: That you were inspired to say something. This person had these malicious, envious thoughts and it seems mysterious how it was healed.

Dr. Hora: The Truth destroys the error of her thinking.

Student: I hear, but I don't understand how it works.

Dr. Hora: How can you be malicious if your guru *(Laughter)* says, "It is good to be good?" You cannot go on entertaining malicious thoughts.

Student: Can't you? *(Laughter)*

Dr. Hora: It is interesting. If I had told her, "Listen, you have to think good thoughts and stop thinking these malicious thoughts," she would have gotten worse, because it would irritate her that I was judging her problem. It is a very subtle thing, because her maliciousness would then be addressed to me. It would become an interaction process where I would want her to stop thinking malicious thoughts to please me, and since she was malicious that morning, it would have aggravated the condition. So, you cannot premeditate your way of helpfulness. It has to be divinely inspired. It wasn't me who was telling her to stop thinking these malicious thoughts. It was just a general statement. "It's good to be good." *(Laughing)* It was like you take an eraser and erase the thoughts.

Student: I see: even for a brief moment if you can see that it is good to be good, there is no place for envy.

Dr. Hora: You keep it nonpersonal. It wasn't me. It was just a general observation, and you cannot resist a general observation unless you are a Talmudist —they take apart everything into tiny comments and it gets completely confusing. There are such philosophers. I think they call them—

Student: Casuists? Casuistic?

Dr. Hora: Nitpickers. *(Laughter)*

Student: The technical term. *(Laughter)*

Student: It seems that what you value has a lot to do with your mode of being in the world, and it appears that there can be a conflict with values from different cultures. You just mentioned that different cultures can have different appreciations of various styles of art. Are styles of art "values?"

Dr. Hora: Cultural values are not spiritual values, and spiritual values are not cultural values. Spiritual values are Christly explanations of reality. Jesus didn't speak about "Jewish values." He didn't speak about "Catholic values." He didn't speak about "commercial values." He didn't speak about "artistic values" He never wrote a poem. He never drew a picture. He didn't make sculptures. But his value system is absolute and infinite and can never be lost. "Heaven and earth shall pass away, but my words shall not pass away." (Matthew 24:35) What kind of bragging statement is that, right? He was in tune with eternal, infinite, absolute Truth, and whenever he made a statement which contained an expression of a certain value, these statements were absolute, infinite, and they would never pass away. There are many discussions today among philosophers and theologians and specialists in science and economics. There are many interesting values of many brilliant people, but they are not relevant to the spiritual values which Jesus formulated. It is important to know this, because so many people claim that the values which they are describing are something that they are not — either in philosophical terms or religious terms or mathematical terms. They never hit the mark. They are very fascinating, very interesting, but they don't hit the mark.

When Einstein expressed one value, and it is a revolutionary idea— $E=mc2$ —this is a mathematical attempt at describing an eternal value. Jesus didn't use mathematical formulations. It'sjust very simple. He said, "The words that I speak unto you arenot mine but he that sent me. As I hear I speak."[4] It is true. So, itis good. It is not only good to be good, it is good to know what

---

4 -"… whatsoever I speak therefore, even as the Father said unto me, so I speak. " (John 12:50)

are spiritual values and what are human attempts at formulating eternal values – either through poetry, or art, or mathematics. Many brilliant mathematicians come up with fantastic declarations of values, when it's just nothing. It's just mathematics. It is not spiritual values. Mathematics contains analogies to eternal values. It is an analogy. It is not the value itself. So, we don't have to be impressed. We appreciate these talented people who can describe certain issues and problems in mathematical terms, but that's not existentially valuable. It is just valuable on the level of human life. One student who comes to another group is a young womanwho has tremendous mathematical talent. She was working fora bank, and they appreciated her and admired her talent. They recently gave her a job of placing 150 million dollars into various investments. Practically nobody has this talent, and she did it, successfully, brilliantly. Four weeks later they fired her. (*Laughing*) She has another job now that she loves as a computer specialist with mathematical talent. These are interesting mental processes, but they are not what we are talking about. They are not spiritual values. They are human values, material formulations about intelligence and usefulness. Because if it were so that these great minds, these great discoverers, inventors, mathematical geniuses were spiritual, they would be enlightened. But none of them is enlightened. Admirable, yes, but they do not see the light. It's very interesting that it is possible to be an astrophysicist, a computer wizard, but that has nothing to do with Divine Reality. If you were to tell them, "Listen, you are such a great mathematician, do you know that it is good to be good?" They wouldn't know what you are talking about.

Student: Suppose you spoke to them about order and symmetry? They are kind of divine attributes. They might be familiar with that, if they were mathematicians.

Dr. Hora: They would appreciate it, certainly. But it would stop there. Now, what is it about an enlightened individual that is different from these brilliant scientists and computer wizards?

Student: I think that from what you describe, the scientists are manifesting intelligence—an awareness of intelligence and ideas. Perhaps they have a receptivity to intelligence, but not so much to love and concern with being beneficial in the world.

Dr. Hora: Okay, now you point out something very important: Without love, nothing is really valid. It is a recipe with the chief ingredient missing *(Laughing)*—nonpersonal, nonconditional benevolence.

Student: If a person is enlightened, is there backsliding? I mean, it would seem that once a person was enlightened, it would be so clear what's what, that there would be no need then to backslide or monitor thoughts.

Dr. Hora: That would be a good question to ask somebody who is enlightened to tell us. *(Laughter)* Can you backslide? What do we mean by backsliding? Suppose an "enlightened" man is embezzling. He works in a bank and he embezzles some money, right? That would be backsliding, but he wasn't really enlightened. He just thought so.

I heard somebody on television speak about spirituality, and this lady was very, very knowledgeable and brilliant, and she spoke about "pop spirituality." Do you know what she meant by "pop spirituality?" She is a student of, *A Course in Miracles*[5]. She spoke about "pop spirituality." That is like pop music or pop art, yes?

Student: Is it maybe something that we want to be instant and quick?

---

5 -New York: Viking: The Foundation for Inner Peace, 1976.

Dr. Hora: Anything that is "pop" means the aim is popularity, right? Even the issue of "spiritual values" can be perverted. There is maybe a motivation to become popular and create an impression in some people's thinking, *Ah, this lady is enlightened.* Maybe not. Sometimes you can talk a blue streak and make the impression that you are enlightened.

Student: Even as you are talking, I am looking at an "enlightened one" as a person. I am not seeing an inspired soul.

Dr. Hora: Yes, as long as you see yourself as a person, you are in interaction with other persons. And that in itself shows that you haven't really understood what the issue is. The Zen master describes the enlightened state as, "Erase yourself utterly." Then you are not preoccupied with Mayor Koch's approach: "How am I doing?"[6] Right? *(Laughter)* That is the antithesis of the truly enlightened individual: "How am I doing?"

I think it is possible to backslide, no matter how. But, we don't really know about Jesus, even though we have various records that say he lost his temper with certain people. He even became assaultive in the temple. He had his backsliding experiences. As long as we seem to be in this body, there will always be backsliding.

---

6 -New York City's three-term mayor, Ed Koch, was known for asking his constituents, "How am I doing?"

4

Group Rivalry

Student: The idea, *What blesses one blesses all*—is that only a spiritual idea? It seems that one has to completely transcend the Four Horsemen.[1] I come across rivalry in corporate life where I work, and I try to transcend malice. I am amazed that no one seems to see that *What blesses one blesses all.* The prevailing view is that if somebody gets something, somebody else feels left out. Is that it? Is that all there is on the human level? Help me. I am struggling. I see a lot of rivalry in the workplace, and it is disturbing. I see the blessings that come my way, but that is not to say that somebody isn't going to try to take them away when that happens. What do I do?

Dr. Hora: Well, in the human world, it is smart to think that one man's gain is another man's loss. It is so logical that any fool can understand it, right? But to live by another principle—*What blesses one blesses the other also*—you have to be a special fool for that. (*Laughter*) Most people don't understand. It doesn't make any sense. It is seen as being stupid or being a "goody-two-shoes," right? Or when we say, "It is good to be good," who will believe us? The world doesn't operate on these principles. They do not apply. The world operates on the principle of the Four Horsemen. The Four Horsemen are the antithesis of everything that Metapsychiatry is teaching.

Student: "Antithesis" means "against"?

Dr. Hora: Yes, the opposite. There is *thesis* and *antithesis*, yes?

---

1 - "The Four Horsemen are: Envy, Jealousy, Rivalry, and Malice." *Beyond the Dream: Awakening to Reality*, Session 56: "How Mature is God?"

Student: That was helpful. Does that mean that in Metapsychiatry we are aware of the rivalry, and we just see it as a lack of understanding, that there is a higher principle at work?

Dr. Hora: Of course.

Student: When we are attacked through rivalry or whatever, what do we do?

Dr. Hora: What you are saying is, "How can I survive in a world where everybody is everybody else's first enemy?" Even your bestfriends, even your family members, are your enemies—they betray you. They are jealous. They wish you ill. They are malicious. Howcan we survive in a world like that? (*Laughter*)

Student: By being immune to it, I guess.

Dr. Hora: Being immune to it. That is good. How do you gain this immunity?

Student: I think it has something to do with whether we share the same interests and motivations that the world is interested in. If we do, then we are not immune.

Dr. Hora: Yes. Suppose you are an executive of a corporation, and you do good work and people say nice things to you and you get raises and bonuses and recognition, and you turn around and behind your back some people are stabbing you in the back by every possible means. What will you do then? (*Turning to a student*) You've worked for years in a corporation, right? What would you recommend to this lady? How can she survive? Jesus said, "Behold, I send you as lambs among wolves." Then he had a recommendation. [2]

---

2 - "Behold, I send you forth as sheep in the midst of wolves: be ye therefore wise as serpents, and harmless as doves." (Matthew 10:16)

Student: Keep a low profile. (*Laughter*)

Dr. Hora: Very low. Okay, but then somebody will say, "Then I won't get anywhere. I will not be promoted. Nobody will have respect for me, and, in the best case, they will think I am a simpleton or something."

Student: Then you are buying into that game. If you have the viewpoint that one will not be promoted or recognized, unless one is self-promoting, then you are in the game.

Dr. Hora: Yes, so you are damned if you do.

Student: I think it is possible to survive and prosper.

Dr. Hora: And prosper in such a work atmosphere?

Student: Yes.

Dr. Hora: Tell us what the secret is, because very few people really know. How do you?

Student: Well, the principle of "nonpersonal, nonconditional benevolence" is a good place to start.

Dr. Hora: Yes, well, how do we do it?

Student: That is not my specialty. (*Laughter*)

Dr. Hora: I was once working in a clinic that was like a corporation. It was full of psychologists, doctors, and others. The mental climate was devastating with the Four Horsemen to such an extent that everybody hated everybody else and was afraid of one another. There was gossip and malicious behavior, which is normal for a corporation; but after a while, people started dying. All kinds of diseases and illnesses befell the people in that corporation. When I saw that, I bowed out, and until this day, that is the secret of why I am still alive.

Sometimes it is advisable to run away. It is the first principle of the karate system. (*Laughter*) The first thing—you run away, and in that system, if you can't run away, then you have to learn how to kill other people so you won't get killed.

Student: Dr. Hora, that sounds strange. Normally you say something to the effect that if you see what is real, it won't affect you. But here you are saying, "Just divorce yourself from it and move on."

Dr. Hora: Right.

Student: It seems more contradictory.

Dr. Hora: (*Laughing*) Well, the Zen master said, "If you meet the Buddha on the way, slay him." That's not nice, is it? The first thing is, you have to have your eyes wide open. I know about a lady who is working in a corporation, and she is always saying what a good friend she has there. She does this and that for herand she helps her to be promoted, and she is so nice. This is her supervisor, and everything seems sweet. In a corporation, the more friendly somebody is, the greater the danger is. It is a jungle out there, and you must not be fooled into trusting anybody in sucha situation, because they will stab you in the back. Neither must you *mistrust* anybody; but you have to have your eyes open. You have to know that the whole structure of corporate life, or hospitallife, or other such environments, is rigged in such a way that everybody is everybody else's enemy, inevitably and unavoidably.If you have illusions or fantasies—*Oh, he is my good friend; we are friends. He is good to me. He gives me all kinds of promotions and recommendations and things* —don't kid yourself. Our whole culture is a very deceitful culture. Of course, the other cultures are also. The elementary mistake of human nature is that it is deceitful and malicious and envious and jealous. The Four Horsemen are operating in every situation. However, if our eyes are open and we know that in this particular setup, nobody can trust anybody, we must not resent it—it is not because people are vicious, but because it is set up that way. So, you try to survive as a spiritual consciousness, not as a "good human person." Our first mistake is to think of others as "good human persons." There is no such thing. *Homo homini lupus.* What does that mean?

Student: Man is like a wolf.

Dr. Hora: Yes, exactly. In ancient times, people knew this. Actually, this is very unfair to the wolves. (*Laughter*) Have you ever seen a pack of wolves in the wilderness? On television I saw a program about a study done about wolves. They live in packs, in families, and they don't hurt each other, and they have a certain hierarchical setup. They have to constantly respect the leader of the pack, but they are not bad to each other. However, in ancient times, people were very much afraid of wolves because the wolves were predators and wild. Human beings were afraid of them, and so they thought that it was dangerous to live among wolves because they thought they were just like people. But people are much more dangerous. As a matter of fact, it is said that humans are the most predatory and violent life forms on earth.

But, of course, wolves and animals don't study Metapsychiatry, and they cannot be transformed into angels. So, we have to learn how to be angels. Here and there you hear about people writing books and talking about angels. What is an angel?

Student: An inspired idea.

Student: Consciousness.

Student: A messenger.

Dr. Hora: A messenger of God, yes.

Student: A beneficial presence.

Dr. Hora: Yes, a beneficial presence in the world is a personification of spiritual qualities, completely devoid of human qualities. So that's what we are learning to be, even if we live in this jungle of the Four Horsemen. The first thing is to understand the process and notto be naive about "nice people" and "not-nice people," "friendly people" and "unfriendly people." Using the ancient perception of wolves, we can say that people will always be wolves; therefore, we have to become something other than ordinary human beings. God never created a human *person.* God created images and likenesses of himself, and God is good.   We are always looking for the good of God and interested in understanding spiritualblessedness. Whether we work in this group or that group, we mustalways remember that we are not human beings. People often say,"But I'm just human," right? Being human is considered a good excuse for all shortcomings. We cannot afford to be human. The moment we identify ourselves as humans, we join the club of the Four Horsemen, and then we have all kinds of complications.

Student: What makes it possible not to be resentful or impatient when you see a situation for what it is to just calmly take it all in without being too much annoyed?

Dr. Hora: We see in Metapsychiatry that all these human shortcomings come to our attention because we have learned about them, but they don't have to come into our experience. There is a story ofa wolf that had been attacking the people in the town where St.

Francis of Assisi was living. When the wolf approached him, he shook hands with it. He saw that this was a wolf, but to him this was just another creation of God. So, we have to learn to be aware of everything. It comes to our attention, but it doesn't have to come into our experience. If you function like that in your job, then you are a blessed individual, yes?

Student: What is the difference between something coming to our attention or coming into our experience?

Dr. Hora: Someone mentioned "transcendence." How do we transcend the evils of the Four Horsemen? First of all, we have to see it. Most people don't want to see it. "I don't want to criticize." "I don't want to see." You try not to see. You start by avoiding looking. That will not work. That will not give you immunity.

Student: It just fills you with lots of fear.

Dr. Hora: Right. One of our students has such a "wolf" at her work— one who is so nice to her, who praises her and recognizes her. Every time she mentions her name, I cringe. How is she going to get hurt again from this "wonderful friend," who is also her supervisor? We have to have our eyes open and see without condemning. We have to see that we cannot condemn. We see without condemnation, and we understand what we mean by "compassion." We have compassion for these wolves in human clothing— "wolves in sheep's clothing" (*Laughter*). We have to see, and then we can transcend it and have immunity. You would be surprised how many people just refuse to look—to see. The idea is, "Well, it can't be so bad. They say nice words, and they are supportive of me, and they bring me candy." So, we rationalize. And there is our enemy right there. But this enemy must be transcended, and if we cannot look at our enemy, we cannot transcend it. We have to be able to see clearly, and then we can transcend it.

Student: I guess the human approach to trying to fix the problem is to avoid it, to look away. Every time you brought this up, I would get a pain in my back, as you know.

Dr. Hora: That is the right place. You are being stabbed in the back. We do not harbor a grudge. We do not resent it. We don't feel victimized. We just see it, and we know this is a human condition and we are not human. It doesn't apply to us, because our life is in God.

Student: It seems to me we would have to be very advanced to be able to transcend it.

Dr. Hora: Well, we are not going to slow you down. You can advance as rapidly as you are interested in doing. Sometimes we fall into the trap of self-righteousness, and we enjoy feeling victimized. We keep complaining: "It's not fair. It's not fair." Nobody gives a damn about *fair* and *not fair*. I remember when a recent President remarked, "Life is not fair," and people immediately picked it up and rationalized their difficulties by quoting the President. What help is it to say that? It doesn't solve anything, right? Life doesn't owe us fairness. God didn't say, "I have created the world to be fair. I have created a fair world." There is no such thing. So, we cannot say, "It's not fair." It's an invalid kind of rationalization to say, "It's not fair." Children often say two things to their parents: "You don't trust me," and "It's not fair!" Who said that I have to trust you? They demand that adults must trust them. It is a trap if you believe *Daddy should trust me* or Mommy, or relatives. We also hear adults say, "You must trust me," and they are quite surprised that we don't. *Fair* and *not fair* is invalid, and *trusting* and *mistrusting* is invalid. It is a waste of time, and it gets you trapped in an invalid idea about life. Nobody owes us anything. Nobody has to trust us. Nobody has to mistrust us.

Student: How else do we cope with life when it seems so unfair and
   lousy?

Dr. Hora: It is only lousy if you allow it to be that way—if you look
   for fairness and you look for people trusting you. I spoke today to
   a lady who bought some expensive jewelry. She bought it because
   the salesman was a nice person. She said, "I know people. I can tell
   character, so I trusted him." She bought it because she trusted the
   salesman, and it turned out to be a terrible deception. In addition, it
   turned out to be a place which was run by the Mafia. So much trust
   she had! She got a second opinion and they discovered that it was
   made with highly overpriced diamonds of inferior quality. When she
   went to return it and get her money back, the salesman threatened
   her, "I will get your children if you make trouble for me." Then she
   was stuck. She had been taken because she thought that she could
   trust this man. In turn, he was threatening her. This lady has had
   several incidents when she has gone to a beautiful store and gotten
   taken in some way because she trusted the salespeople. She didn't
   know how to live in this jungle without trusting or mistrusting. She
   found herself entangled in a dangerous situation with a Mafia-like
   character who also called her fiancé to threaten him. Of course, they
   lost the money. It was an expensive lesson, because this guy
   threatened her—if she was going to demand the money back, he
   would do something hurtful to her.

That is another situation where someone is looking for fairness
and for trust. But if we are not expecting people to be trustworthy
and fair, then we are forced to take a different perspective on the
situation. God has given us intelligence, and either we understand
what we are doing and nobody has to do us a favor or we don't
understand. We need to understand what we are doing when we
transact business. If we don't understand, it is not good to transact
the business until we understand what we are doing. Then there are
no problems. When we have difficulties in life, usually we ask for

it. Nothing comes into experience uninvited. Human ignorance and credulity have no limits.

Did you see the television show last week called, *The Crusaders*? It showed an effective way of presenting a problem to doctors. They went into doctors' offices and hospitals, and first they found out whether the doctors were forthright and well qualified. In every instance they found that the medical personnel were cheating. They were greedy, they were not qualified and didn't know what to do. It was a frightening picture of the lack of ethics and qualifications of these doctors and nurses.

Student: Were they chosen at random, or were they selected because they were good stories?

Dr. Hora: It was an investigative program. They investigated a number of people in private practices and in hospital practice, and made abhorrent discoveries about insensitivity, greed, fraud, and lack of knowledge, and mistakes. There was a doctor who was performing an operation, and in the middle of the operation he ran out of anesthetic, and he had to go three miles to the next pharmacy to get more anesthetic and while leaving the patient in his office in agony. Unbelievable situations. Unbelievable! Then there was a case where the patient was being shunted from one doctor to another, which is often done, and every one of these doctors had a different diagnosis. Finally, the person came to a confidence-inspiring doctor who said, "What you need is an operation to take out the prostate. We'll do it right away." They prepared him for the operation, and then the patient said, "Hold it a minute. I vaguely remember that I already had this operation a few years ago." (*Laughter*)

Student: So, if we are expecting fairness, if we are expecting people to be forthright and honorable, is that how we invite a bad experience?

Dr. Hora: We have to start way ahead of this perversion. We have to be so clear about the meaning of our problems that we never get to the point where we have to rely on human advice and human help.

Student: Whether it be a doctor or whether it be in the workplace.

Dr. Hora: In business, too. We must constantly rely on God, and not just in terms of "I pray" and other religious terms— "I was a good boy, and now I need help." We have to live such a life that we understand the meaning of every problem and then we don't have to be at the mercy of people, whether they are doctors or nurses or specialists.

Student: God works through others. Isn't that so?

Dr. Hora: Well, of course. How do you know? Was God working through that guy who wanted to perform that prostatectomy?

Student: No.

Dr. Hora: Some people say, "Well, God will protect me from this doctor or dentist, making sure that he knows what he is doing;" but some people are in terrible situations, because a layman cannot evaluate the qualifications of a doctor. No way. Just like I cannot make out my own income tax. Really, we are in such a situation. We sign documents we don't understand. It's terrible. It is really unfair! (*Laughter*)

Student: Quite often, though, you hear people say, "In order to function, you have to have a certain trust." If you keep on mistrusting everybody, you will be so tied up in knots.

Dr. Hora: Of course. It is a terrible mistake to be mistrustful.

Student: And it is a mistake to trust too much.

Dr. Hora: It is a mistake to *trust*.

Student: So, if you don't trust or mistrust, you just, what, observe it?

Dr. Hora: If you are an observer you do both.

Student: So, if someone is your accountant and doing your income tax, you have a certain amount of trust that he is doing it honorably.

Dr. Hora: Well, if you have a certain amount of trust, you can wind up being hurt.

Student: What is the solution, then?

Dr. Hora: (*Laughing*) What does one do?

Student: We are counseled to trust in the Lord.

Dr. Hora: Exactly. How do we do that?

Student: I think earlier you referred to it by saying that we are given intelligence and given the ability to pay attention to that intelligence, and when we evaluate situations on the basis of PAGL, for example, that is a pretty good guideline to the fact that we are seeing things correctly.

Dr. Hora: Yes. In other words, there is no other recourse but God. Without a clear sense of being in harmony with the will of God, we are insecure, anxious; we make mistakes and suffer the consequences. Some say that life has become so complex that it is impossible to have a sense of assurance. The important thing is to know the difference between *certainty* and *assurance*. What's the difference?

Student: "Certainty" sounds more like a human thought, whereas with "assurance" you have a sense of knowing that all things work together for good.

Dr. Hora: Trusting in God, right. Our forefathers knew it, and even on our currency we have "In God We Trust" imprinted. Not in the judges, and not in the lawyers, but in *God* we trust. We have to cultivate this tremendous consciousness of God's power and presence and benevolence, which is always there, though we don't see it. If you practice trusting in God in every step of your life, you will see that there is something wonderful, liberating, and comforting. It is easy to lose sight of it, and when things work out well, we are pleasantly surprised.

Student: Regarding this idea of *fairness*, someone might say that life is not fair. Things seem fair or not fair from a typical perspective. For those that don't know God, that's all there is.

Dr. Hora: Right.

Student: So, is there any way to give someone comfort?

Dr. Hora: No! (*Laughter*) In order to get comfort from somebody else, we have to rely on somebody else, and do you trust that somebody else is closer to God than you? Again, we come up against this dilemma of trusting and mistrusting.

Student: I am still arguing the point. There are many people, on the human level, who are very trustworthy, honest. I am just kind of struck by the point this is an honest person and I can rely to some degree on him as reliable. Is that also suspect? (*Laughter*)

Dr. Hora: The Bible says, "Trust in the Lord with all thine heart, and lean not unto thine own understanding. In all thy ways acknowledge him, and he shall direct thy paths." (Proverbs 3:5) Now, why does God want us to acknowledge him?

Student: So that we are aware of Reality.

Dr. Hora: Yes, that's right. Then we keep in mind that there is a God. He is benevolent. He is omniscient, omnipotent, supreme, intelligent—then we have something to lean on, and it proves itself valid and effective. If we don't have that, we have nothing. We cannot rely on anything else but God.

Student: Whenever we attribute any quality to an individual, we are involved with a wrong judgment. We are judging by appearances.

Dr. Hora: Yes.

Student: And we are also relying on that if that is all we are giving someone—any kind of judgment in order to trust them.

Dr. Hora: Sure.

Student: What is the difference between *leaning on your own understanding* and really discerning if there is an intelligent understanding?

Dr. Hora: We pray and study and keep our consciousness pure so that we can have discernment. We can actually be aware of God's presence, supporting our lives with His benevolence and goodwill. We have to be able to sustain this discernment, and as long as we are aware of this discernment, things work well. We are safe, and we have a sense of assurance. Now, many religious people would like to have certainty of God's love. Today somebody told me that a friend visualized that Jesus Christ loves her, and this gave her a certain sense of assurance. Jesus Christ came to her in a visualization and she believes that this is really a sign from God that Jesus loves her. In the religious life there are certain pitfalls. You are fantasizing that there is a tall man who loves you; therefore, you are safe. You have visualization, you have fantasy, you have dreaming, you have wishful thinking, you have all kinds of mental processes with which you try to find a certainty—that you are safe in this life. And if you rely on imagination, visualization, this or that, you are just spinning a web of superstitious beliefs about yourself in a quest for something tangible that cannot be touched. Have you ever touched an intangible object? That's what it is, right? So again, it is a human dilemma. But our humanness must be transcended.

Student: You said, "Our humanness must be transcended." What is it that has to be transcended?

Dr. Hora: It means that you don't fantasize. You don't daydream. You don't use imagination. You don't use visualizations. You don't use little trinkets and objects and superstitious ceremonies with which you are constantly trying to comfort yourself, because this is self-deception. It is delusion. It has nothing to do with Reality. You have to give up the quest for certainty and understand God to the point where you have a sense of assurance through *awareness*. We have to cultivate an awareness of the reality and omnipresence and omnipotence of God. The more clearly we are able to be aware of this, the more comfortable and free of fear we are, and things work very well. Sometimes to our great surprise.

Student: So, a sense of assurance that *God is* is what we really need.

Dr. Hora: Yes. To that end, we have been inspired to define prayer as *a sincere contemplation of the Truth of Being.* Now, this is entirely different than any kind of religious system or recommendation.

Where in the world have you heard of prayer as "a sincere contemplation of the Truth of Being?" Recently I came across a little booklet about the philosophy of Chuang Tzu. I have spoken to you about Chuang Tzu many times before. I was amazed to what extent Chuang Tzu had the same understanding. He never uses the word "God." It doesn't exist in his vocabulary. He arrives at an understanding of the Tao. The Tao is an intangible, invisible, incomprehensible entity that, when understood, is exactly what we call "God." When you understand God in terms of the Tao, there is no difference. It is a cosmic power, a harmonizing principle of the universe. And how does Chuang Tzu pray? He doesn't use beads or visualization. In his meditation, he seeks to become aware of the Tao. Every moment when you become aware of the Tao, which cannot be defined, cannot be formulated in terms of anthropomorphic images, It is there. As Jesus said, "I and the Father are one. I am in the Father, and the Father is in me." (John 10:30; John 14:11.) The word "Tao" goes beyond the word "God," because it is hard for you to think of God without expecting that somewhere there is some form, and the Tao is totally nondimensional. If you understand the Tao the way Chuang Tzu understands it, you are *there*. And when you are there, a certain surprise comes into your life—mainly spiritual blessedness, because things begin to work together for good, totally uncontrolled and unplanned, unimagined. You just find that this is a perfectly harmonious, generous universe in which you live, and you will be alive after you are dead.

5

Beyond Winning and Losing

Student: Dr. Hora, recently we talked about the idea of rivalry in the workplace and other situations and the importance of recognizing it. Since then I have been giving it thought, and it is becoming clear that rivalry is very much present, in spite of how I have not wanted to see it, address it, or discuss it. I have been physically losing my breath. It is overwhelming. I was at my parents' house during the holiday, and it's been so long since I've had these symptoms so regularly. It just came out of nowhere. Suddenly I felt like I couldn't breathe. I can't always discern the thoughts I'm having at that moment. I try to change my thought, but then when it gets bad, I get fearful. I am struggling.

At my parents' house I immediately started to feel a sense of pressure. I was able to see that there has always been rivalry between my father and me. Interestingly enough, my father disclosed some of his memories of his childhood, and he was also indoctrinated with rivalry in his family context. So, it was very clear. Then the suffering subsided, because I was able to see the issues. He was taught that. He taught me that. I could move on, but I am not completely free of the symptom.

I am becoming aware, but I wake up in the middle of the night, and it is now becoming so consistent that I'm frightened. I know there are thoughts here that I need to see, but I still have to work and function. Today I was in the office and moving into a bigger space. People were acknowledging that I have grown, and I see the rivalrous thoughts coming my way. I start hyperventilating and I can't breathe. I need help. I recognize it. I regret being a part of it, but I don't know what to do with it from this point on. Physically it's very uncomfortable and I am overwhelmed. I really need help.

I never saw myself as rivalrous, but I could see my level of participation. I could see I wanted to be important. There is a duality that inevitably involves the Four Horsemen.[1] I just don't know where to go from here.

Dr. Hora: What is she describing? Anybody? First, we have to know the meaning of these symptoms. You call it "rivalry."

Student: Well, it's a pressure. We talked about the symptoms before. It is some form of oppression. Feeling oppressed.

Dr. Hora: Yes. Who is oppressing you?

Student: Who? Someone I must be rivalrous with. It must be rivalry. Well, you have been telling me over the past years that I have been working very hard to get my father's approval.

Dr. Hora: Yes.

Student: It's a no-win situation, and I know I have not wanted to acknowledge that. I have been working very hard to avoid it. I think maybe this is the issue that must be taking place and that I am not fully aware of it. The symptoms tell me there has to be something. Is that true?

Dr. Hora: Anybody?

Student: Dr. Hora, does that mean that in the human condition, rivalry has a purpose? I mean, when she was describing the meaning, that sounds like cause and effect, but its purpose was to get Dad's approval or acceptance. Is that the way the dynamics of it work?

---

1 - "The Four Horsemen are: Envy, Jealousy, Rivalry, and Malice." *Beyond the Dream: Awakening to Reality,* Session 56: "How Mature is God?"

Dr. Hora: It could be that, but there are all kinds of rivalries loaded with meanings.

Student: Because if we thought, *Well, okay, now it's time for us to be healed of rivalry,* we might get scared—

Dr. Hora: Oh, yes.

Student: —because if we stopped being rivalrous, we wouldn't get whatever goody that we were trying to get from being rivalrous. We all suffer from that, I am sure, and maybe it has a function. And if we would understand the function, then maybe it would help us to be healed.

Dr. Hora: Well, what is the reward of this kind of rivalry?

Student: Is everything that was described just wanting something?

Dr. Hora: Of course, it would be good to know what you want, and that seems dangerous. What do rivals want from each other?

Student: Victory.

Student: Submission.

Dr. Hora: Submission?

Student: It was a little bit confusing, because she was describing how she says she felt rivalrous toward her father, and yet she has also described where she is seeking her father's approval.

Student: Well, I am not rivalrous with him that I am aware of.

Dr. Hora: You're not?

Student: I am? *(Laughter)*

Dr. Hora: That is one way of solving this problem. It's *his* problem. If it were just his problem, you wouldn't suffer. *He* would suffer.

Student: You are seeking his approval.... Right? More than competing.

Student: Right, exactly.

Dr. Hora: That's what makes it so complicated.

Student: So, in wanting something from him, that puts it in the realm of rivalry?

Dr. Hora: So, you have another word for it?

Student: No. I am getting confused.

Student: Where does rivalry come in? I don't understand the word "rivalry" in that situation.

Dr. Hora: That's a good question. Can there be love if there is rivalry?

Student: What are you rivalrous about? I mean, it has nothing to do with wanting love or attention or approval, unless you are rivalrous with your father's attention to your mother. I mean, that would be rivalry. Your sister would be the rival.

Dr. Hora: Here is a student. She wakes up at night in a panic, in fear of dying. Now, you live in the business world and you're exposed to all kinds of friends and foes and competitions. Well, if you are in competition with somebody, you just want to be better than they are. But if you are in rivalry with somebody, what do you want?

Student: To destroy or hurt them.

Dr. Hora: Exactly. You want to eliminate the rival in one form or another; therefore, that situation is present in consciousness. The thought is, *Here is a man whom I want to love, and I want him to admire me, and he wants to brag about what a wonderful daughter he has, and I want that also.* Underneath these thoughts, what is wanted?

Student: To be the best?

Dr. Hora: Destroy one another. Destroy completely; whatever the rivals cherish, they want to destroy in one another.

Student: Does that mean I also want to destroy him?

Dr. Hora: Of course. Didn't you read the papers? There was a woman who cut off the penis of her husband? Do you know about that?

Student: Yes.

Dr. Hora: Rivals want to annihilate each other. How many times did you tell your father about your progress in business? And he refused to hear it.

Student: Right.

Dr. Hora: What does it mean when we are telling somebody something important about ourselves and they pretend that they didn't hear it? What is it? It is annihilation. Now, you have this desire to annihilate a loved one, and you can go crazy about it, because how can you be a loving daughter and a rival at the same time? Especially when there is this element of self-righteousness. What is self-righteousness? Everyone who is afflicted with the disease of intellectual superiority—we call it "self-righteousness"—is a mortal enemy, and secretly we want to annihilate them. There are quite a number of incidents reported recently in the news about some parents who have killed their children. How is it possible that a mother and a father wind up killing their child? What does it mean? When the mother and the father are afflicted with the disease of self-righteousness, they either kill each other or they kill the child.

It becomes *vitally* important to win, but if you are in rivalry with an infant, you cannot win, because the infant will scream and scream and scream until he drives you out of your mind. Have you ever heard of little infants who are driving their parents crazy with the screaming?

Student: Is that what a colicky baby is?

Dr. Hora: Well, people think it's a physical issue, not mental, or, they think that if it *is* mental, it's the child's problem, not the parent's. We *do* get enmeshed in murderous rivalry where nothing matters but winning, and we cannot win with a baby. We cannot stop a baby from screaming because the baby has been sucked into a power struggle.

Student: Is the power struggle between the parents and the baby? It just seems so incredible to me, because the baby is so innocent.

Dr. Hora: Yes. Innocent, but the catch is: *What do the parents want?* The parents demand quiet. "Be quiet!" And the more you want to control the screaming of the child, the more the child will scream. Yesterday I saw a television show where there were two sets of teenagers and their mothers. The mothers and the TV host were trying to get these teenagers to participate. All kinds of struggles were going on in those families, and the teenagers discovered a secret weapon to enable them to win, and they were applying it, and the parents were being driven out of their minds. The mothers went all the way to this show in the hope that they will get the children to reveal themselves as bad children. The children's secret weapon was stonewalling. Do you know what "stonewalling" is? What is it?

Student: Well, my son does it. *(Laughter)*

Dr. Hora: What do you think? He has discovered this for himself, that he can refuse to respond to his parents and just sit there. It drives them crazy, because he deprives them of their urge to control, and the parents become completely helpless. And how can parentsput up with that? Right? The secret weapon is non-responsive stonewalling. It was pointed out that the children on the show were stonewalling. They just sat there like they were made of stone, and no matter what anyone said, no matter what they were asked, the children were silent and said nothing. So, the TV host and all the guests and everybody in that room, were going out of their minds, because they didn't respond. They said nothing. They were like Brazil nuts. *(Laughter)* Have you ever heard this term? A Brazil nut is so hard you need a hammer to break it open, and even then, you may not be able to. When there is rivalry, it gets worse and worse, until everybody becomes paralyzed, because the beginning of rivalrous situations is the desire to win, to prove oneself strongerand to be able to control the other. So, colleagues want to exert pressure to control each other, and parents want to control their children. Wherever there is somebody involved with another individual, where the control of one another becomes the issue, you have a malignant situation of extreme tension and rivalry on acontrolled secret level.

If parents believe that children should be controlled, psychologically, then for years there may be a tremendous tension, until it explodes into violence. And when the violence takes over, then somebody gets hurt physically. So, essentially, the problem in rivalry is that somebody is self-righteous. Suppose there is a man who thinks he knows everything better than anybody else, and has the power to make you agree with him, and you refuse to agree. Suppose there is a father who is a male chauvinist and he cannot tolerate a woman being smarter than he is. And if that woman is a daughter or a wife or a neighbor, it doesn't matter, except that there is this hidden agenda of who will win. Who is stronger? Who is right? Who is smarter? This is going on, and it can go from bad to worse, and this is called "self-righteousness" and "power madness" and "rivalry." It can be intellectual rivalry. It can be economic rivalry. It can be fame. Who is more famous? Who is smarter? Who is better? Who can exert control on somebody else? There is an awful lot of suffering, whether it is on an intellectual level or a very low level of so-called "relationships." Relationships are a problem, andthere is a lot of anxiety. It's interesting. There can be one hundred people in a place, and among these one hundred people, there is one individual who is power mad and self-righteous. The whole place gets sort of overtaken by the insanity of self-righteousness, and pretty soon everybody is competing with everybody else and is clashing. In finer circles, this is called "debating." But it is a murderous kind of warfare over control. And this can be in politics; it can be in family life; it can be in corporate life. People can get sucked into this warfare anywhere, and there is a lot of suffering. It is a dangerous situation, because some people just go to pieces. They can't take the pressure, and it is totally unnecessary, because what do you win when you win?

Student: The annihilation of the other.

Dr. Hora: Well, it can be symbolic and it can be just silent. Among primitive people it can come to fights. There are always fights. People are killing each other, but there is always latent anxiety.

Student: Wouldn't you win your own sense of superiority? Isn't that the goody in it?

Dr. Hora: The goody?

Student: If I defeat the other person I prove my own superiority.

Dr. Hora: Anything. Anything. When there is rivalry, there is warfare. It can be psychological. It can be emotional. It can be gender inspired. Nowadays it is very fashionable for women and men to get involved in the desire for mutual annihilation. It is called "anxiety," but nobody knows how to stop it. It can go on and on, and it is very harmful. How do you extricate yourself from such an engagement in a life-and-death struggle? It is always a life-and-death struggle. You cannot just say, "I will stop it." You cannot stop it; you see it and you cannot go on with it. It is killing you, and you cannot stop it unless somebody helps you to see the real issue: self-confirmation at the expense of another.

Student: In other words, the child then wants to annihilate the parents?

Dr. Hora: Of course. He wants to win. He doesn't want to be controlled.

Student: So, it's a matter of winning for survival.

Dr. Hora: Right. He gets killed in the process, and this is going on everywhere, in families and in jobs.

Student: I'm confused. I can see the drive to not want to be controlled— no question—but I can't see having any malice toward them, because I don't. I don't blame them.

Dr. Hora: You can love them, but you want them to drop dead. *(Laughter)* That is the insanity of rivalry. All rivalries are an engagement in a murderous, so-called relationship.

Student: That's built into the idea of rivalry.

Dr. Hora: Yes. Yes.

Student: But isn't it recognition that she is seeking not so much rivalry with her father? That she is just seeking recognition?

Dr. Hora: The father also wants recognition. He is a very successful author and successful economically. He is a very intelligent fellow. He has proven himself to be of superior intelligence and success, and he is respected in the community, except by his wife. *(Laughter)* On an intellectual level this is called "family life." Of course, what is needed is a complete understanding of our purpose in life and what is really good.

Student: It seems that I can't really understand Perfect Love unless consciousness is cleared of all issues that relate to this.

Dr. Hora: Thank God you are here; otherwise, you would never know until you drop dead. *(Laughter)* But even here you have people who become hardened in this battle, and we call them, "Brazil nuts." *(Laughter)*

Student: Is it her fear of dying, when she wakes up with the anxiety?

Dr. Hora: Yes. That's what it is. She is afraid that the father will win and it will completely destroy her. That is what is called *pavor nocturnus*. What is that? Not even she knows. *(Laughter)* What does *pavor nocturnus* mean?

Student: Something that happens at night?

Dr. Hora: "Terror in the night." It is the fear of not being able to survive this pressure for control.

Student: Losing your breath is losing your life.

Dr. Hora: Yes. Exactly. That's what it means. It is very important to get out of this morass of involvement, this interaction involvement. The Bible says, "Come out from among them and be ye separate." (2 Corinthians 6:17) But it is hard to come out, because the other party will think that it has won. *(Laughter)* And this is not acceptable. *(Laughter)* Are we crazy or aren't we crazy? *(Laughter)*

Student: Do we have to go through that? Do we have to let them win?

Dr. Hora: Do we have to let them win? You have to *lose interest* in the whole issue of winning or losing. There is really no such thing as winning or losing, and we have to see through it. "Ye shall see the Truth and the Truth shall set you free." (John 8:32) Nothing else. You have to see that winning is not an option; neither is losing an option. The only option is Perfect Love.

Student: Rivalry takes two, so if one is able to step aside, then there can't be any more rivalry.

Dr. Hora: You cannot step aside, because the other party would say, "I won."

Student: Hopefully we don't care.

Dr. Hora: What does that do? "Hopefully?" No, you have to reach a point where you can clearly see that *winning* is not an option and *losing* is also not an option.

Student: This is really helpful, because I notice one thing about my mother, my sister, and me growing up with my father: we all have this defensive, combative way of being with him. We are always protecting ourselves. Recently I noticed at work that I always have to fight for certain things. I am so tired of fighting, and certain things have fallen away where I no longer have to fight. But now I hear you saying is that it's all part of this way of constantly fighting to be in control.

Dr. Hora: Yes.

Student: And when I talk to my mother, it's hard to have a conversation with her. She is always defensive. She is always combative.

Dr. Hora: Right.

Student: At least now I can see the dynamics of it and how it has affected each family member in being with him. That is very helpful. I found that all those battles were annoying, but they were annoying because I really didn't understand them.

Dr. Hora: That's the sad part. When you are in this power struggle, you don't understand. You think you have a breathing difficulty. You have a physical symptom. If you think that this is a physical symptom, you never get out of it. You get worse and worse and worse and using more and more tranquilizers and all kinds of drugs against this fear of dying for lack of breath and air, but that is not really the issue. That is just a side issue. So, it is very dangerous to win, and it is impossible to lose. The whole thing is insane. You have no place to turn. Here and there, there are some very intelligent people who can extricate themselves through avoidance. They are not healed, but they found a way to avoid the war. A student has a very brilliant child, a boy, and he found a way of escaping from taking piano lessons. How did he escape from the battleground of the piano lessons? He secretly picked up a trumpet, and he became a masterful musician of the trumpet, and nobody knew it. *(Laughter)* The parents were completely surprised. So, it couldn't develop into a war. Now he is blowing and he is happy, and the parents sit there in amazement. *(Laughter)* He is really an exceptionally brilliant boy and he was able to save himself this way, but most people would say, "I would rather die than let him win."

Student: One of the events that happened, and I don't know if it's valid, because you have often told me to keep my mouth quiet,but my father started to complain about my mother while I was hyperventilating. He didn't know it but I was trying to maintain my peace and he was complaining about it, and I said nothing. I had learned not to say anything to him. And then I said, "I can't help you. There is nothing I can say," and he said, "I am not asking for your opinion. I am just asking for someone to listen to me." I said, "Okay. Have you ever considered how you got yourself into this?" He said, "What do you mean?" And I said, "Well, it takes two to tango. It is not just one-sided." Then he said how good he is at this, that, and the other. I said, "Yes, but you have no respect for women, period." And with that, he didn't say another word.

Dr. Hora: And there is no answer to that. Who in the world would lower himself to such a degree as to have respect for a woman? You cannot tell somebody to respect a woman.

Student: So, he wouldn't even acknowledge that.

Dr. Hora: No. No.

Student: So, it doesn't matter. I don't have to say anything.

Dr. Hora: The way to be healed of this problem, to be rescued, is to face up to the fact that there is no such thing as "winning" or "losing."

Student: So, the issue is taking control. That's the main theme there.

Dr. Hora: Wanting control.

Student: Wanting control. Because everyone is fighting for control for survival.

Dr. Hora: Yes.

Student: And this falls under the realm of rivalry.

Dr. Hora: Rivalry, yes.

Student: So, if I could see these aspects, then that is the only way out.

Dr. Hora: You have to save yourself. Literally, you have to save your life. How do you save your life? It is to completely abandon the interest in winning or losing.

Student: Replacing it with what?

Dr. Hora: With the love of the Truth. Truth is not a personal possession, and anybody who thinks he is able to say, "I am right," is insane at that moment, because there is no such thing as a human person being right. Unless you are willing to give up this fantasy, that you are right and others are wrong, you will never be liberated from this hellish, burdensome problem. It would be enough just to say, "I am not right. I cannot be right. Nobody can be right, and I am not interested in being right. No matter who says what, I am not interested in being right."

Student: It would be enough to say that?

Dr. Hora: If you *sincerely* can make that statement, at that moment you give up forever and ever the great pleasure of saying, "You see, I was right." If you want to save your sanity, and if you want to have peace and sleep at night comfortably, you give up this foolish desire to believe that you can be right about anything. And then a little voice will say, "But if I give up being right, then they will claim that they are right." Right? Nobody is right, and then you have peace, yes?

Student: It wouldn't matter if we gave up the desire to be right and somebody said they are right, it wouldn't make any difference to us.

Dr. Hora: Absolutely nothing. We would feel sorry for that guy.

Student: My mother always has this expression, every time she says something, she says, "Am I right?" And she will wait for the answer. *(Laughter)*

Dr. Hora: So, the enlightened response is, "Whatever."

Student: If we are not a person who is right or wrong, what is the Truth?

Dr. Hora: The Truth is *there are no persons.* Nobody is right. The Truth is the only Truth that is, and besides the Truth, nothing matters. You don't argue about who is right, because there is no such thing as somebody being right. Once I spoke to a self-righteous mathematician who was a student of Metapsychiatry, and I said to him, "2 and 2 is 4," and he said, "More or less." *(Laughter)*

Student: A long time ago I was a counselor at a camp, and the director was a big man. He didn't realize it, but he was very willful, and these little children, who were disturbed, would have temper tantrums all the time. He would try to make them stop having temper tantrums and the more he would try, the more they would scream. He would scream, and nothing ever worked. This went on day after day after day. He would never admit it, but it was clear that no progress was ever being made with these children.

Dr. Hora: Yes. He was a Brazil nut. *(Laughter) (A child is heard screaming and crying in the background, and there is more laughter.)*

There is a student who has a mother who is obsessed with the issue of success and failure, and she has always been pressuring her daughter to be successful. Consequently, the daughter is always getting fired and losing jobs and can hardly make a living. She goes to school and fails the examinations. She is an intelligent girl, but she is under pressure from her mother to be a success and she is constantly failing. The mother thinks she is a loving mother. She wants good for her daughter.

Student: So, in this scenario of the pressure of pushing the daughter to success, how does that invite failure? I don't understand that, if she is intelligent.

Dr. Hora: If she is successful, the mother wins. Who can stand it? *(Laughter)* But you see, your dad doesn't mind it if you are successful. He just doesn't want you to be more intelligent than he is. When you tell him that you passed the exam, you say, "See, father, I am more intelligent." Some people value success, and some people value intelligence. Some people value money—who makes more money, *et cetera.*

Student: So, certain dualities are more important to us than others. It depends on which one we have been indoctrinated in.

Dr. Hora: Yes. There are specific specialties within the scope of craziness. *(Laughter)* You can pick and choose how you want to win.

Student: So, the real bottom line issue is *winning.* It doesn't matter the context. It's just winning. Winning and being right.

Dr. Hora: Right.

Student: Do we think we will die if we don't win?

Dr. Hora: We can think almost anything. The problem is thinking. If we understand the nature of our craziness, then there is a good chance to be healed. But you always have to understand the meaning of the problem.

Student: You said earlier that rivalry has a meaning. The meaning is whatever is the control issue.

Dr. Hora: Exactly.

Student: I can see I still have things I have to sort out. This doesn't necessarily mean the symptoms will go away, so I wake up in the middle of the night.

Dr. Hora: As soon as you let go of the desire to be right, you will sleep like a baby. If we cannot sleep, it is a sign that we have some craziness in our thoughts. So, you can just repeatedly remind yourself, *I am not interested in winning. I am not interested in losing. I am not interested in letting somebody get a bigger bonus than me. I am not going to think about that. I am only grateful to God, who reveals to me the nature of human craziness so that I could be healed of it and have peace, assurance, gratitude and love. It doesn't matter what Father thinks. He can think that I am a winner or he can think that I am a loser.* That is the hardest thing to give up.

Student: By that you mean resisting him.

Dr. Hora: Resisting him. The meaning of the resistance is wanting to be right in any situation. One of our students, a lady, has an employer who is in the business of selling items, and he would rather lose business than let her think she has sold something. *(Laughter)* He is in business to sell things. No! *(Laughter)* He would rather be right. *(Laughter)*

Student: I notice that if I read an editorial or listen to someone on television who is saying something that I think is wrong and that I am right, I get upset. That's because I think I am right. It never occurred to me until now. It all sounds very innocent. It's been happening lately that I have been getting very upset and feeling symptoms. It never occurred to me it was because I was so sure I was right and they were wrong and I didn't have any way of proving it. How free you are if you don't have that problem!

Student: I don't understand. What's the answer to that? If you listen to somebody and you think that they are wrong. *(Laughter)*

Student: But Dr. Hora just showed us that nobody's right and nobody's wrong.

Student: I mean, I hear it. It doesn't register. *(Laughter)*

Dr. Hora: That is what it is with your dad. You tell him a thousand times that women deserve some respect.

Student: If somebody says to you, "Today is summer." You say, "No, you are wrong. It's spring." There is a right and there is a wrong.

Student: You think so. *(Laughter)*

Student: Maybe the problem is you don't insist on it. If you think it's summer and I think it is spring—and it is spring, not summer —*(Laughter)* I still don't understand. What is the escape out of this bind?

Dr. Hora: You have to lose interest in being right.

Student: But if it *is* spring? *(Laughter)*

Student: Would it be helpful to say he has the right to be wrong?

Dr. Hora: Yes. That is very helpful, except then already you are back in the "he and I." Now, the Zen monk who was accused of kidnapping a baby had the right solution.
He said, "Is that so?" [2] Period.

Student: To be able to attain that. To be able to say, "Is that so?" is really being enlightened.

---

2 [This] story is about a very saintly Zen Master, living in a cave above the village. In the village there was a young girl who became pregnant. In her distress she made up a story that the Zen Master was the father of her child. When the child was born, the villagers became incensed and took the child and dumped him in the Master's lap, accusing him of being guilty of this shameful act. When the Master heard these accusations, he looked around and said, "Is that so?" and accepted the baby without protest. Years passed and the young woman had a change of heart; she confessed in the village that she had lied about the Zen Master, whereupon the villagers became incensed again, and a crowd of angry men and women came to the Zen Master, accusing him of keeping the child unlawfully for himself, whereupon the Zen Master, having listened to their accusations, said, "Is that so?" and returned the child. *Beyond the Dream: Awakening to Reality*, Session No. 42

6

Success

<hr>

Student: Would you expand on the word "benevolence"? I usually think of it as a way to approach people. I wonder if you could go into it a little bit—the meaning of benevolence.

Dr. Hora: It means "to wish well." It comes from the Latin, *benevolentiam.*

Student: But I am sure the spiritual meaning is much more than that, more than the common use of the word.

Dr. Hora: It is "good will." That's all. No problem with it. The Italian phrase is *Ti voglio bene*— "I wish you well." Next time you pick up an Italian girl, say to her, *"Ti voglio bene."* (*Laughter*) You will have it made. (*Laughter*) It's a beautiful language. The Italians are very amorous. You want me to explain that word? (*Laughter*)

Student: Benevolence towards another individual is still a human quality, right?

Dr. Hora: Only if a "human being" says that.

Student: If you are not spiritually minded and if you are not seeking to understand perfect love, then it is human. But inherent in that, there are always the Four Horsemen.[1] Benevolence doesn't seem to

<hr>

1 - "The Four Horsemen are: Envy, Jealousy, Rivalry, and Malice." *Beyond the Dream: Awakening to Reality*, Session 56: "How Mature is God?"

exist on a human level. Unless you have some spiritual idea, it's not really there.

Dr. Hora: Yes. Now what is the problem with that?

Student: I am disappointed that there really is no true goodness on the human level.

Dr. Hora: On the human level, there is "good and bad"—inseparably joined together—two sides of the same coin. Now, those who live in spiritual Reality have no money. (*Laughter*) Their wealth is in unequivocal good will. The good of God is spiritual blessedness. Spiritual blessedness has no flip side to it. You could say there is cursedness. It would be the flip side of this, but God doesn't curse anybody. In some religions they curse people, but God doesn't curse anybody. God is love. There is no flip side. Therefore, we can quietly make the statement "The supreme good of life is spiritual blessedness."

Student: All spiritual qualities are spiritual blessedness. If we understand any of the spiritual qualities, we are learning what spiritual blessedness means.

Dr. Hora: Yes. It is pure goodness. As we say, "It's good to be good."

Student: That was very helpful for me when I first learned about it. I was recently away visiting someone for a couple of weeks and that idea carried me through—*it's good to be good.*

Dr. Hora: Yes.

Student: It's good to be good. Is it the same thing you once told us about the idea of love? "We are loving because God is love."

Dr. Hora: Yes, we are friendly because God is love.

Student: So, *being good to be good* is the same idea, because God is good and spiritual blessedness has no flip side.

Dr. Hora: Sure. Yes. Many people spend a lot of energy on cultivating friendships, right? Have you noticed that? Everywhere it is considered a good idea to cultivate friendships. It seems okay. What could be wrong with that? Anybody?

Student: It's all interactive.

Dr. Hora: Yes. That's correct, and what's wrong with that?

Student: Always making deals. (*Laughter*)

Dr. Hora: What do you think about that? Could it be that it is not a very good idea to cultivate friendships?

Student: Well, it seems to be a good idea looking at it from a human perspective, but the main thing friendships probably do is take you out of Reality and put you in a dream world, and that's very troublesome.

Dr. Hora: Some people are shocked when they hear that to cultivate friendships is not a very good idea.

Student: It involves having a relationship and an attachment, and we know that's troublesome.

Dr. Hora: Yes.

Student: So, "being friendly" is much different from "cultivating a friendship" or "having a friend."

Dr. Hora: Exactly. We are friendly because God is love, and we understand, more or less, that we are transparencies for God. So, all the qualities of God constitute the truth of our being and we continuously pray, sincerely contemplating the Truth of Being.

Student: It's so easy to be knocked off our focus. I wasn't here for one week, and I really got tossed around.

Dr. Hora: Yes. Tightrope walking is very precarious, isn't it? (*Laughter*) Now, to some of us being on the spiritual path is like tightrope walking. Have you noticed?

Student: The Bible says, "Strait is the gate and narrow is the way." (Matthew 7:14)

Dr. Hora: Yes. How can we find a better, more solid path than a tightrope, right? What makes it so precarious, being on the path? Do you know the story of the rabbi who found himself in hell with a bishop and a Christian Scientist? The three of them were in hell, and they were feeling sorry for themselves and talking to each other. "How did you get here?" "Why are you here?" So, the rabbi said, "I know why I am here. In our neighborhood there is a butcher, and he had delicious ham in his window. Through the streets you could smell the aroma of this freshly baked ham. I couldn't resist it and I ate this ham. So that's why I am here." They turned to the bishop and asked, "Why are you here?" He said, "Well, across the street from my parish there lived a lady, Mrs. Calabash (*Laughter*). She was so beautiful, and I couldn't resist her." So then both of them turned to the Christian Scientist and said, "Why are you here?" He said, "Who, me? I am not here." (*Laughter*) This is apropos of the tightrope. Everybody walks on a tightrope until the time has come that he really accepts the truth that *it is good to be good.* As long as it is an effort to be good, we are on a tightrope. So, we fall off the tightrope, but we have to scramble back up again.

Now, why should anybody bother with this if it is so difficult to be a saint? Why bother to be pious or religious? Not many people really bother. To most people it is a lie, hypocrisy. But some sincere people are really struggling very hard to stay on the tightrope. Now the question is, why do you bother?

Student: It seems, that once you embrace the path, it doesn't seem like you could live life any other way. You can get thrown off, but anything on a human level is never healing. It's never helpful. It's never permanent. It's so precarious that you want to get back on and keep walking. It just doesn't seem that life could be lived any other way.

Dr. Hora: Yes. Many people think that all you need is a drink or a drug or a pill.

Student: But you always have to pay a price. There is always a price to be paid.

Dr. Hora: A pharmaceutical one. (*Laughter*)

Student: You pay a price on the tightrope of the spiritual path, too. It's not all "easy street."

Dr. Hora: Well, if it were "easy street" we wouldn't have to talk about it. You are talking about the fact that it is so difficult to stay on the path without sliding off.

Student: But did you also say that if we are enlightened and we really realize who we are, then there is no tightrope?

Dr. Hora: Right. All you have to do is just get enlightened and you have got it made. (*Laughter*)

Student: But if you really understand, there's no struggle anymore.

Dr. Hora: No struggle whatsoever.

Student: But then we wouldn't be here anymore. (*Laughter*)

Dr. Hora: It's easy to speak about enlightenment, but it's not easy to attain that kind of realization where we can say, as Paul did, "None of these things move me." (Acts 20:24) What did he mean?

Student: He meant that we are buffeted around by ignorance. You can transcend everything that isn't real.

Dr. Hora: Yes. As long as Mrs. Calabash attracts you, you are not yet enlightened. (*Laughter*)

Student: Sometimes it's very human that people might want to succeed on a spiritual path, because it's another way of being successful or gaining a certain measure of fame. It could turn into a human goal, so to speak.

Dr. Hora: Yes. But you see, as long as we have a desire to be successful, we don't really know what we are saying. On that tightrope there is no such thing as "success" or "failure."

Student: Or "winning" or "losing."

Dr. Hora: Right. Many people have certain preconceived notions about this process of becoming enlightened, and they don't succeed, because unconsciously they think that you have to be successful at it or you have to win. These are certain preconceived notions from the human experience, that to become enlightened you have to work and you have to do certain things and become successful at it. It is not possible to become "successfully enlightened." (*Laughter*) And when we talk about it we immediately see the validity of this point. It is not a matter of being successful or failing. Oh, we can succeed at being failures. That's easy. But it is not a matter of success or failure or winning or losing. It is very, very confusing, and we can easily "chase butterflies" and get nowhere for years.

Student: If it's not a matter of winning or losing, what is it a matter of?

Dr. Hora: Sincere contemplation of the good of God, which is spiritual blessedness. You cannot succeed in this. If you seek the good of God, you cannot be successful. It is very frustrating, isn't it?

Student: We cannot be successful in what measure? I don't get it. (*Laughter*)

Dr. Hora: It's hard to get it.

The whole idea of "success" doesn't apply in the quest for spiritual enlightenment. You cannot succeed. So why bother? Many people just chuck it after a while.

Student: You've said in the past that what's required is interest. It's easy to be enlightened, it's only difficult to be interested.

Dr. Hora: Right.

Student: In order to be interested, we really have to understand its nature and its value.

Dr. Hora: Yes. Correct.

Student: So, all that is really needed is to be interested.

Dr. Hora: But who is interested?

Student: Well, you wouldn't be interested unless you appreciatedthe value of it—that the other ways of being, that other interests, pursuits are ultimately frustrating.

Dr. Hora: Okay. (*Addressing another student*) Now what do you say to that?

Student: I don't know. It puzzles me.

Dr. Hora: Well, what you see here is the business of suffering. Suffering is a two-by-four which is hitting us over the head until we become truly interested. When we have suffered enough and tried this and tried that and blamed this one and the other and nothing works and we are miserable, we can reach a point where we see that we just want to win. We just want to be successful. We just want to have a handle on God. We want to do it right.

Student: There's that word "want."

Dr. Hora: There is a lot of suffering going on, and it's hard to be interested in something so abstract, so intangible, so elusive, as the good of God. It sounds good, but how can you be sincerely interested in the good of God to the point of excluding everything else?

Student: That's the big issue, because generally when we are interested in something other than what we are talking about now, we like it or it catches our attention, or somehow we are attracted in some way. We call that "interest," but that's not what you are talking about.

Dr. Hora: Right.

Student: You're using the word "interest" to the exclusion of everything else. That means to the exclusion of everything that you ever thought or believed or were taught by the world, and it takes a long time to come to understand what you mean when you say "interest." So, I can think that I am very interested, but it's obvious that when I dwell on other thoughts, I really am not interested in the good of God, because if I really were interested in the way you are speaking, I would be here for God one hundred percent.

Dr. Hora: Yes.

Student: I finally realized what you meant when you suggested it to me in a private session with you last week. You described the experience of my being torn between gratitude and pride when something good occurred in my life. There appeared to be this tug between recognizing God manifesting and personal pride. I was considering the word "pride" during the week and I realized what it is. Pride is believing that I was successful in achieving that good.

Dr. Hora: Exactly. Yes.

Sometimes if we are healed of a serious problem, we know that we have to be grateful to God for being healed, but there is an undertone of another idea which is, *I did it. I did it with God. I prayed right and God did what I wanted him to do.* Then you say, "I am grateful. Thank you, Father." But underneath you are congratulating yourself that you succeeded and you even like to tell your friends about it, and that is called "a testimony." (*Laughter*)

Student: Or you can take pride in the fact that, *Gee, I must be advancing spiritually.* (Laughter) You can take pride in that.

Dr. Hora: Yes. The human being is very screwed up. (*Laughter*)

Student: Is what we are talking about "giving up the human endeavor?"

Dr. Hora: Absolutely.

Student: Also, we can't really exclude an interest in either, because that is another form of human endeavor.

Dr. Hora: What do you have in mind?

Student: "Mrs. Calabash." If we see that we have an invalid interest and say, "Well, I am not going to do that anymore, I am just not going to think about that"—that's still human endeavor. Doesn't sincere interest take us away from it so we are not doing it anymore? It's the interest that's moved us away from Mrs. Calabash.

Dr. Hora: Of course. We cannot heal ourselves, but the sincere interest in the right idea of God and man will bring about a clarity where these problems do not exist. We have the impression that we have accomplished a healing. We cannot accomplish anything. "By mine own self I can do nothing. It is the Father who dwelleth in me. He doeth the work." [2] If I really mean it. (*Laughing*) If I am sincere. We have defined prayer as *the sincere contemplation of the Truth of Being.* The Truth of Being is that God is all in all, and we are consciousness. If we have learned that, then it totally absorbs our interest, and then surprising things happen. We cannot be proud of it. We cannot take credit for it, and if we are grateful, this gratitude has to be absolutely pure.

Student: But realistically, the sufferer is actually interested in alleviating his or her suffering. That seems very clear. It seems we have to go through the process of suffering to a certain point where we transfer

2 - "I can of mine own self do nothing." (John 5:30)
"Believest thou not that I am in the Father, and the Father in me? ...the Father that dwelleth in me, he doeth the works." (John 14:10)

our interest away from the alleviation of suffering. I can't see how we could continue to suffer and at the same time have a sincere interest in the contemplation of the Truth of Being. There seems to be some sort of a trap here that I don't quite understand. If I am suffering, I would like not to suffer any more and I would like to somehow be successful in applying my studies to alleviate the suffering. That sort of describes what I am going through. So how can I be sincerely interested in the Truth of Being?

Dr. Hora: You are telling us that you assume that it is all right to have a desire to escape suffering. Is that a valid desire? It immediately throws a monkey wrench into your whole work. How can we have a desire not to suffer if God doesn't know anything about it? We cannot desire suffering and we cannot desire *not* to suffer. We can be interested in *what truly is*. Consider the fact that millions of people are filling the hospitals throughout the world and they have all kinds of painful diseases and are suffering terribly, and the doctors cannot do anything about it. There is a lot of suffering in the world and nobody has the answer. How can people be helped to escape the suffering? Sure, it's natural if we have pain we want to be free of the pain, but that's the devilish part of it, because, if we have a problem, we want to do something about this problem so that it wouldn't hurt us. So, the moment you are trying to do something about your problem, you are trying to interfere with God, and it doesn't work. It is natural to desire to be healed or to be relieved of our suffering. Suffering people throughout the world are mentally preoccupied with how to escape from suffering. Interestingly enough, medical science thinks that the more we know about suffering the greater the chance that we will find a way to escape it, but all along we know more and more about the problem and we don't have the answer.

It stands to reason that the only way to deal with problems is to confront the problem and say, "This *seems* to be a problem, and I am not going to get involved with it. I will be involved with *what really is* and I will focus my attention on understanding Reality.

I am not going to speculate about the fine points of all kinds of diseases." The question is, "What is what really is?" Years ago, Heidegger came up with this question. He said that we have to focus our attention on the question of *what really is*, because sickness, suffering, tragedy, pain and illnesses are not what really *is*. So, the more we desire to be relieved of our suffering, the worse it gets. No wonder, then, if someone has a pain somewhere in his body, or in his bookkeeping, the more he tries to immerse himself in figuring out how to escape, the worse his problem gets. You may have heard of people who were quite tolerably all right, and then they went for a checkup by a doctor and were sent a to hospital, and there they got worse and worse. The "physical examination" has caused a lot of trouble for people. The remedy is not to be sidetracked by studying illnesses or problems, but to be absolutely interested in the good of God, which is spiritual perfection, freedom and blessedness. Now, it is easy to talk about this, but the fact is that if you look at the world you see that people are suffering and there is not much help. Usually they get worse, and wherever they turn they have some problem, so then they naturally turn to a specialist. But *we* say that you have to turn to somebody who knows that *there is no problem*. But that is not easy.

Healing is not a conquest. Healing is the discovery of spiritual perfection, discovering *what really is*. Perfect Reality, perfect God, perfect man, absolute freedom, perfect Love really *is*. But who is interested in that when you have a stomachache? (*Laughter*)And yet that is the only way to find the solution, because all our sufferings are just hooked on unreality one way or another. Neither regular medicine nor alternative medicine, nor drugs, nor this nor that help us to get out of this mesmerism. Joel Goldsmith says that every illness is a case of hypnotism. We get hypnotized and we don't know how to get out of it. The only way to get out of problems is becoming *sincerely* interested in contemplating the Truth of Being. This means you have to lose interest in everything else.

Student: I get hung up on the idea that I am not going to get involved with the problem, and I'm thinking to myself, "You have to be strong." Then I don't get involved with the problem, but neither do I turn my attention to what you were describing. I just sort of stay there in limbo, being strong.

Dr. Hora: "Being strong" is also an illness. It's also a lie, and that's not a solution. There are people who are struggling against illnesses. Many people are being strong and fighting it. People are told, "Fight it, don't give in," and it just reinforces the hypnotic belief that we are sick. How can you be "not sick" if you feel sick, right? But if you contemplate with utter sincerity the Truth of Being every day, every moment, every chance you get to completely focus on the nature of Reality, you may become so familiar with the Truth that you will have no problems in your life. There will be nothing to heal or to correct or to medicate.

If you watch television, you are constantly barraged by various sicknesses and their pharmaceutical remedies. People are preoccupied with their aches and pains, and they listen to advice on what to do in order not to have this problem. In one ad two young ladies are talking, and one says, "I have a splitting headache," and her friend reaches into her purse and pulls out a bottle of pills and says, "Take two." (*Laughing*) Everybody has treatments for whatever ails them. People are afraid of suffering. There is so much fear in the world about these terrible diseases. Whoever heard about AIDS before a few years ago? And no sooner is one problem corrected in some way than two other problems arise. Millions of dollars are being spent on finding remedies. The world is in a real mess if you look at it on the basis of how it appears to be. The real remedy is to look at it how it *doesn't* appear to be. (*Laughing*)

Student: The media present it in a way that is different from our day-to-day experience.

Dr. Hora: The media?

Student: For example, I don't really hear people talking about taking pills, but in these commercials they are pushing the pills. It's in the media that these ideas are really as popular and dominant.

Dr. Hora: But there is a market for it. You know that. Supply and demand.

Student: Even where the need isn't there to begin with, they promote it.

Dr. Hora: Oh yes, sure.

Student: So, people are prompted to think that they don't sleep well or have some other problem.

Dr. Hora: They are really promoting the illness on the excuse that they are giving relief. It's all messed up. You watch television and the advertisements and they are blatantly lying all the time. Respectable people are paid a lot of money to go on television and lie. Lying about some product—this has become so widespread that people don't even notice that they have sold themselves and their integrity down the river. They are being paid to lie. The commercials are really corrupting the nation, because if you can lie for ten thousand dollars, next time you will lie for five thousand dollars. We have to admit that real healing requires a great deal on the part of anyone who is interested in it, and it is something that cannot be done. We have to accomplish that which cannot be *done*. It requires sincere interest in the Truth of Being, to the point where we begin to see that Reality is flawless and perfect, and that suffering and disease are self-inflicted states of consciousness.

Student: How do I get out of the trap of my attempts to not engage in thoughts about the problem—the trap of trying to be successful in not being mesmerized by the problem or afraid that if I am not successful I am going to continue to suffer?

Dr. Hora: I just explained to you that there is only one remedy that Metapsychiatry has evolved in understanding: *the sincere contemplation of the Truth of Being*, regardless of all the distractions which the world is throwing at you. The sincere contemplation of the Truth of Being has to go on ceaselessly. It is called "ceaseless prayer." [3] You have a headache. Turn your attention to the Truth of Being and don't dwell on your headache, and within a few minutes there will be no headache. There will not be a memory of having had a headache.

Student: What about the meaning of the headache? I thought that looking for the meaning of a problem is a tool to understand. [4]

Dr. Hora: It is a tool, if you know how to use it. Sometimes you get enamored by your meaning. Then you dwell on that too much.

Student: You said you have to know how to use the tool? How do you use it?

Dr. Hora: Well, first of all you have to remind yourself there must be a meaning to this problem. That reveals to you a certain thought process, and it can also reveal to you your mistaken efforts at healing yourself. Once you know the meaning, then you can let go

---

3 - "Pray without ceasing." (1 Thessalonians 5:17)

4 - "In all our work in Metapsychiatry we ask two questions: (1) What is the meaning of what seems to be? and (2) What is what really is?" *Beyond the Dream: Awakening to Reality,* Session No. 1: "What is Man?"

of it and turn your attention wholeheartedly to the Truth of Being. Yes?

Student: Not to become enamored with it or hold on to it.

Dr. Hora: Right, exactly.

Student: What's the meaning of wanting to hold onto it?

Dr. Hora: It's the desire to conquer the problem. It's very frustrating when we have a problem and we don't know the meaning of this problem and we just wrestle against it and try to conquer it. We are not conquerors. We are blessed manifestations of Infinite Mind.

Student: When we find ourselves ruminating over a problem—

Dr. Hora: That means that we want to conquer the problem.

Student: That means we want to be successful.

Dr. Hora: Right.

Student: You're saying that if we have pain and we are sincerely interested in understanding the Truth of Being, then we will see whatever we need to know, whether it be the meaning or the right idea. The meaning may not be revealed at that moment, but the right idea will manifest itself.

Dr. Hora: Yes. Right.

Student: Then that will be transcending the pain.

Dr. Hora: Yes.

Student: I always thought that you had to understand the meaning before you could see the Truth, but if we can first see the Truth, and the meaning can follow because we may not have been receptive until then.

Dr. Hora: Yes.

Student: I get caught up in the fear of the pain. I think I have to know the meaning, because I am suffering. But if I understand what you are saying, if the Truth of Being is the focus and I dwell on that, somehow that seems comforting. Is that right?

Dr. Hora: These questions indicate the desire to have a handle on the problem. Because sometimes we can find several meanings when we ask, "What is the meaning?" It is not like a surgical procedure— "spiritual surgery"— which you apply to your own problem. (*Laughter*) Whatever will help us to appreciate the Truth of Being, that will be the best and fastest way to find that we are all right. There is no headache. There is no problem. Nothing is lost that cannot be found.

Last week I went to the hardware store to buy some lightbulbs and then came home. Later I discovered the shopping bag had no light bulbs in it. (*Laughter*) I went back to this store and that store—all the stores that I'd been to that day, and nobody knew anything about the lightbulbs.

Student: Did you leave it in the oven? (*Laughter*)

Dr. Hora: Something similar. I went home and I let go of it, and then I looked in the closet, and there they were, carefully put away in their rightful place. I gave up trying to solve it, and it turned out that all those trips I had made to the stores were unnecessary. (*Laughter*) So I wasn't negligent. I just stopped forcing my will on the problem and stopped dealing with the problem. You see, trying to solve problems makes them worse. We have to let go and let God, because God is the only Mind, the only Intelligence, the only Reality, but we don't believe that. We like to think, *What about me? I am a smart guy. I should be able to remember where I left these bulbs*, right? (*Laughter*)

7

Sex, Companionship and Marriage

Student: Can I bring up a situation I spoke with you about but I haven't resolved? Briefly, I met a girl a while back and I got attached to her, and things seemed to be going all right until she said, "Let's be friends." So, I spoke to Dr. Hora about it. I was upset that she would take that course of action. Sometimes, for a reason I can't explain, this seems to be all right. Then I can swing over the otherway and get very angry and resentful about the whole thing. I just want to wipe my hands of the whole situation. It's back and forth. I don't understand what's the thought of that swinging from here to there.

Dr. Hora: Yes. Well, if a girl wants to be a friend, that's an intolerable insult.

Student: Right. (*Laughter*)

Dr. Hora: What makes it so?

Another Student: It's a personal rejection. It's just that she doesn't want to have sex at that particular time in the friendship.

Dr. Hora: What do you think about that?

Student: I don't think that's the issue.

Dr. Hora: No?

Student: No. There wasn't anything before that. There was no sex before that.

Student: No. I didn't mean that. I think that when a lady says that she just wants to "be friends," it means that she wants to get to know you and to be friendly with you, and then see what develops.

Dr. Hora: She is offering companionship.

Student: Yes.

Dr. Hora: And this is an insult?

Student: She could mean what was said. It could be meant as an offer for companionship. But I think a lot of women, if I understand it, use it as a rejection. It's intended that way.

Dr. Hora: Yes. If you are a sex-starved bachelor, or have this in mind right from the beginning without saying so, then of course you feel rejected and you suffer frustration. It's a miserable thing. Who wants companionship? You want to fuck, right? (*Laughter*)

Student: Maybe I'm kidding myself, but I don't rule it out. (*Laughter*) I think it's probably more of an issue for somebody to like me or accept me, than it is to have good sex or sex at all. I could be kidding myself. I don't rule out sex, but I think it is more the issue of finding someone you like and they like you. Someone you get along with.

Dr. Hora: She seems to have respect for you.

Student: But when she said, "Let's be friends," that took it down.

Dr. Hora: It depends on your view of friendships. What is your idea? What value system do you bring to this? How can an offer of friendship be a rejection?

Student: Because it's noncommittal.

Dr. Hora: She is committed to be your friend.

Student: And friends with anybody else too. (*Laughter*)

Dr. Hora: So you only accept the friendship providing she writes off the rest of the world.

Student: Because otherwise I am just another guy.

Dr. Hora: You are not? You are not just another guy?

Student: I'm just saying, if she keeps it as just a friendship, and things are still open socially, then I am just another guy. I have had this in the past. She is not seeing anybody else. I think her approach is, *He's a nice guy. Let me go out with him. We go to nice places. I enjoy his company and he's all right for the time being until "Mr. Right" comes along, and then I will leave him for the guy I always wanted.*

Dr. Hora: What is it you really want?

Student: I want me to be "Mr. Right" to her.

Dr. Hora: For how long?

Student: I'm not getting any younger. (*Laughter*)

Dr. Hora: No wonder women hate men.

Student: Dr. Hora, I worked most of my life in the bar business and I can say he's right that men find this difficult. If a woman does say she just wants to be friends, it's a bit of a put-down. It's likehe says, you feel like you are being pushed aside. You feel like it'sa rejection. It's a coded way of saying, "I'm not attracted to you." Men find it difficult to be friends with women. There generally seems to be an underlying attitude that if women are friendly with you, they are interested in you physically. Men can have men friends but usually not women friends.

Dr. Hora: But this is a lovely, decent girl who doesn't play games with men and doesn't drag them along with a ring in their nose and exploit them. She is very sincere and upfront about what her desire, her lifestyle, would bring her in this situation. I think she deserves a great deal of credit and respect for being forthright and doesn't fool around and promise something she knows she has given up long ago. She is 54?

Student: She is 52.

Dr. Hora: She is a sincere Catholic and a very intelligent woman. She thinks that because you are Catholic, too, you have a right to expect more than companionship from her. That would be a mistake. I think she is absolutely right. But somehow that does not correspond to your fantasy life about women. You see them as sexual partners. There are bullshit artists, both on the male and female side, but it is very rare to find somebody like this woman who is forthright and sincere and upfront and very pleasant to be with and doesn't exploit you in any way. It is very surprising how you insist that there must be sex in that situation. I think you really deserve to have a bitch for a woman who will really let you have it. (*Laughter*)

Student: Never in all my life, and I am in my 50s, have I ever heard of a situation that a man meets a woman and they go out with the understanding that they're interested in being just friends. I never even heard anyone tell me that.

Dr. Hora: Isn't Metapsychiatry wonderful?

Student: Well, it's new. (*Laughter*) I can see a boy and girl who are 18 or 22 and they meet. They are too young, so they say, "Let's be friends." But when you're in your 50s and you meet somebody, who says, "Let's be friends?"

Dr. Hora: 18, 20s – they don't know anything. They just go by their sexual desires. They are being exploited, and they are exploiting. We hear this all the time. People make each other unhappy and miserable because they have certain expectations and fantasy lives. Sex is the outstanding issue with such inexperienced people. There is nothing more beautiful than true companionship with positive regard towards each other. That's the nicest thing that can happen. To you this is not interesting. It's a rejection. It is *not* a rejection. It is a gift of God.

Student: I can't see how you can say it's a gift of God. I see the logic. I hear the words. It's something inexplicable. I protest that it's a gift of God, and I don't see it. It upsets me that this is the way it turned out.

Dr. Hora: God has a wrong arrangement for you. (*Laughter*)

Student: Maybe I will learn something.

Another Student: It's so hard when we are growing up. It seems we have so many expectations, female, male, sex, companionship, friends. I know when it came into my experience I didn't understand it. Often, I said to Dr. Hora, "What do I need this for?" Dr. Hora said, "It's a blessing. God is blessing you." I kept thinking about that, because it was so easy to feel rejected and disappointed. It wasn't like I thought it would be. *What will people say? What will my parents say?* There was so much garbage that had to be eliminated! I just wanted to give up, but Dr. Hora would say, "It's God's blessing." I was suffering, and I'd say, "What?!" It'shard to understand when we have thoughts that we aren't awareof, but here is an opportunity to look at them. Eventually I think that there is a shift in interest. We lose interest in some of these ideas, and then we can see the value of a companionship. Sex, if it comes, it comes. If it doesn't, it's secondary. The primary thing is the harmonious coexistence and coming to understand what thatmeans. Getting older it gets lonely; it's difficult. As Dr. Hora often says, "How romantic, dividing the workload!" (*Laughter*) I startedto appreciate different ideas and thoughts that I never imagined, that I never thought could be possible, and there is great value to that. I think it's worthy to explore the misconceptions, because itreally is a blessing to be in a companionship, and there is an awfullot of growth there, and if this woman is interested, boy, that's a real addition.

Student: At first, in the very beginning of the conversation, there were two analyses of what "Let's be friends" could mean, and I think that could be something that he might really want to explore and ask her, "Do you really want to be friends, or are you just saying 'See you around'?" I was thinking that for eight or ten years, when I was single, one of the issues that was a problem for me was that I really did want to be friends, and it was the men who said, "Well, if all you want to be is friends, then forget it." So then there is the night you want to go out to the movies and there's nobody to go with, and it seemed like there was almost a bargain that had to be struck, that if you wanted companionship it seemed to come loaded with a romantic element. I couldn't be more in agreement with the idea that any good time that you spend with someone, good companionship is the main ingredient. If this lady really wants to be friends, it could be a blessing to you both, and it is also perhaps the way in which this can grow into something, this could turn into something more. The interesting thing is, I think so many people put the cart before the horse. They get the romance and the commitment ahead of the companionship, whereas in a long-term marriage, the companionship is really what sustains it.

Dr. Hora: Right, sure.

Student: By the way, I have been telling this to my son for the last 48 hours. (*Laughter*)

Student: Are romance and friendship mutually exclusive?

Dr. Hora: Yes, romance is a situation of mutual insanity (*Laughter*), whereas companionship is mutual respect, and that is most satisfying. Insanity is never satisfying. It has ups and downs and recriminations and misunderstandings and a lot of anxiety. That is not a solution. It is a misdirected mode of being in the world.

Student (addressing student): Do you think that you have a sense of what this woman does mean when she says, "Let's be friends?" Was it a way of saying, "Let's not see each other anymore," or was it a way of saying, "I would like to maintain a friendship?"

Student: She says there is no electricity. She uses very romantic words. (*Laughter*) We went to see the movie *Shadowlands* about C.S. Lewis and his wife. It was one of those tearjerkers. She's crying away about everything romantic.

Dr. Hora: That's not romantic, that's sentimental.

Student: She says, "There is no passion." "There is no electricity." "Let's be friends." She's very kind. Maybe I made it sound a little harsh. I'm an old-fashioned guy. I have a one-track mind; I am pursuing a certain direction because at my age I haven't got time for "friends." I have to get right to it. (*Laughter*) I take this as a traditional rejection. She told me she has done this to some other guys in the past. She likes to cultivate friends.   She is interesting to be with, but it's just that I was looking for something more than being kept at arm's length. I don't know, but I suspect there might be something more there. She needs a little, as they say today, "space" to think things out and slow things down.

Dr. Hora: You are still hoping?

Student: I can't get it out of my mind. *All right, I'll play the game of friendship in the hope that somewhere down the line….* This is the way I think; otherwise, why go out just to be going out like friends. I have never done that before. It's all new.

Student: Try it; you'll like it. (*Laughter*)

Student: My point is that if a girl is not interested in you, what's the sense of going out with her? This is what I have always believed. I have never heard guys talk any other way. I don't know. Wouldit be a mistake to think that if she and I were to become friends, it might lead to romance? I hate to use the word "romance," but I can't think of anything else. In other words, am I supposed to be friends with her just to be friends?

Dr. Hora: Yes. So? Isn't that important?

Student: Not really, because, well, she is nice to be with but —

Dr. Hora: You can go to a whorehouse.

Student: You keep bringing up the issue of sex. I wouldn't think of going to a whorehouse.

Dr. Hora: What else are you talking about?

Student: If I go to a movie, I go by myself. If I want to go to a concert, I go by myself. I have been doing it for years. I travel by myself. I do everything by myself. If it means anything to me, I usually do it by myself. So I can keep on doing it by myself.

Dr. Hora: In fact, you never really understood the joy and the blessing of harmonious coexistence in a companionship.

Student: I have with guys, but it's never that way with women. It's always been: you date, and if you are not interested in each other, you just don't associate with each other anymore.

Student: Being friends doesn't mean that someone is not interested in you. The interest is just different. It's qualitatively different.

Student: It's insulting. (*Laughter*)

Student: What makes us want sex? What is the issue there?

Dr. Hora: Hollywood. If you want to have a family and children, then it's all right to have sex, but in Hollywood they present sex as a form of entertainment. That's the only rationale for this kind of life. You are using each other to build a family, to have children, until you abuse each other and you have these tragic situations where everybody suffers. The children suffer, the husband suffers, the wife suffers, because you are just using one another in a material, salacious, sensual way, and the results are very bad. Just look around and you will see it. Only those married people who have discovered companionship – only they can hope to have a blissful family life.

As long as a husband and wife are just using each other, they will always be abusing each other, and there will be misery from the woman and the man and the children and the mother-in-law, etc. It's a mistaken idea that men and women are here for sex. They are here to have family life or to have harmonious coexistence in the form of companionship, shared interest, shared values. How do we say, "division of labor?" (*Laughter*)

The wife does the shopping and the husband does the cooking. (*Laughter*) One of our friends married a man who is a gourmet cook and she is not allowed to go in the kitchen. (*Laughter*) Hollywood says that sex is essential, because without that life is boring. It is an important form of entertainment. Indeed, whenever we have a preconceived notion about what is important, if it isn't there, we feel deprived and bored.

Student: An individual might have preconceived ideas about a relationship and his or her partner also has certain preconceived demands. It's impossible for harmonious coexistence because each one has preconceived notions about the way things should be, and that makes it impossible for anything good to unfold according to God's will.

Dr. Hora: Sure. That's right.

Student: Even if nothing is ever said, you have expectations or silent demands. There is no freedom. Every individual must have the freedom to be here for God without any constraints from another person.

Dr. Hora: It's always amazing to watch how eager people, particularly women, are to get married. There is a tremendous urge to get married, and invariably they wind up extremely unhappy and troubled. It becomes a "should." "I am already 30 years old and

I am still not married!" There is an urge, a rush to marry, because if you are not married, you are considered nothing by others. It's our "should" thoughts which pervade the culture, and everybody thinks that this "should be." A "should" thought can never lead to happiness and harmony. Just look around at your friends and relatives and ask yourself, "Which one of them is happily married?" Nobody. (*Laughter*) And I happen to know quite a few who are in a privileged position. If there is sex, there is no happiness. If there is no sex, there is also no happiness. Some of them complain about being pressured into sex, and some of them complain about not having sex. So everybody is a loser. If you have sex or if you don't have sex, you are a loser. How is that possible? Because in the universe of Mind, there is no such thing as "wanting something" and "hoping to be happy." You cannot want anything. We can *be* what God wants.

Student: I guess when you say that companionship is a blessing, it's an opportunity for us to manifest harmonious coexistence, which is what God wants.

Dr. Hora: That's what God wants, because that's what God *is*. When we are what God is, this is bliss. This is called "spiritual blessedness." The First principle of Metapsychiatry says, "Thou shalt have no other interests before the good of God, which is spiritual blessedness." How many marriages do you know where both partners are seeking to realize spiritual blessedness? Do we all know what "spiritual blessedness" means?

Student (who had asked the opening question): Maybe we could go over it again? (*Laughter*)

Dr. Hora: You are interested now? (*Laughter*)

Student: Yes. (*Laughter*)

Dr. Hora: It looks like we are making headway. (*Laughter*) "Spiritual blessedness" occurs when everything works together for good.[1] It's an unfolding of God's will for us. It can include sex, but it is notthe primary issue. In some people's lives having children is very important and it is acceptable, but also not absolutely necessary. Many people have children for the wrong reasons, with wrong motivations and invalid fantasies. Just like some men want to marry a good-looking woman so that they can go to a bar and show off the lady on their arm. This is their motivation for marriage! Have you ever heard of such a thing? Some people get married just to show off the girl when they go to the bar. (*Laughter*) Some other people have some other fantasies about how to gain respect from the community. But all this is absolute nonsense and only leads to suffering.

Student: I don't know how it works. It's like a mystery, but if you don't want anything from each other, then there is harmony. It's that wanting sex, or anything, that's destructive.

Dr. Hora: We are here for God. We are not here for ourselves, we are not here for a group, we are not here for particular people, and we are not here for an occupation. We are here for God. We need to grow in appreciation of companionship and harmonious coexistence. That is the only way that we can live with each other and enjoy it. Everything else is just troublesome. There is a couple, Masters and Johnson[2], who developed a scientific study about sex. They wrote several books. When they were younger they were just romancing together, but later they got married, and after they got married, everything went wrong, and within a few years they divorced because they couldn't live together. They had a system of

---

1 - "And we know that all things work together for good to them that love God, to them who are the called according to his purpose." (Romans 8:28)

2 - William H. Masters and Virginia E. Johnson.

training people how to have sex, and if the marital partner couldn't learn the trick, they supplied the married people with alternative partners to practice how to have sex with them. The whole thing was ridiculous, and nothing was accomplished. In the meantime, they became renowned for the scientific study of sex. They would manipulate each other's genitals and all kinds of things, and they called it "scientific sex." They are famous. They thought that by teaching the technique of sexual intercourse, they could help people to become happily married. Of course, it didn't work. Has anybody heard about them lately?

Student: They recently held a conference. I was surprised. For some reason they have gotten back together to give a conference out West.

Dr. Hora: Conjugal bliss can only come from mutual respect and appreciation of companionship —and division of labor. (*Laughter*) It is very nice when you have a wife and a husband working together preparing meals, raising children, educating them, building homes, *et cetera.* This is life. This is the good life.

(*Dr. Hora singing*) "Once you have found her, never let her go."[3] (*Laughter*) (*Addressing the student who asked the opening question*) I think you have found a very nice lady if you could appreciate her. You and I have gone through quite a number of ladies. (*Laughter*)

Student: I've left a trail. (*Laughter*)

Student: In the context of us discussing the beauty of companionship, it sounds like he is saying that mere companionship with a woman isn't of interest. It is possible that practicing companionshipis a route to romance or marriage, not as motivation, but as an opportunity to understand companionship as one of God's blessings and to actually have this experience with a woman.

---

3 - "Some Enchanted Evening", by Oscar Hammerstein II and Richard Rodgers. 1949.

Dr. Hora: Sure. Sure. You don't have to reject sex in marriage or out of marriage, but you just have to understand its rightful place. If it is absent, it's no problem. It's no tragedy, as long as there is companionship, the sharing of a mode of being in the world.

Student: But is it true that a woman could say that she wants to be friends and really mean it as rejection?

Dr. Hora: Yes, rejection comes in many interesting varieties. This is a field to fascinate psychologists. "How many ways can one person reject another?"

Student: Whether or not you can decode what this woman said, it just seems that a valid way of approaching the opposite sex might be the practice of companionship, as opposed to dating. Your idea of dating seems to be categorized into this one area where you take somebody out and talk with them and have a structure which is basically romantically loaded.

Dr. Hora: Then the question is popped, "Your place or mine?" (*Laughter*)

Student: My thing is, I think if you get along with someone of the opposite sex, sharing interests and all that, it seems only natural to me that you go to the next step.

Dr. Hora: What is the next step?

Student: I just can't see getting along nicely with some woman and never thinking of romantic involvement. It just seems strange to me.

Dr. Hora: Shakespeare said, "There is nothing neither good nor bad but thinking makes it so."[4] When you start thinking, you lose

---
4 - *Hamlet*, Act II, sc. 2.

everything. It becomes a "should." When we start thinking about relationships, marital or otherwise, then everything turns into a "should" or "shouldn't," and that's the end.

Student: This woman really does want to go out with you again?

Student: She seems to. She wants to set the context of affection.

Student: I don't really see that as rejection. I know when I was younger and I was dating and I wasn't interested in somebody, I might say something like that not to hurt their feelings. It was just a nice way of saying, "I don't want to see you anymore." I wouldn't continue to go out with them. I would say that if we were in school together, when we could conceivably be friends without going out.

Dr. Hora: She wants to go out with him. It's not a final thing.

Student: Then the wheels start turning in my mind, and I think, *Why is she so interested in pursuing a friendship with me?* I can only believe that maybe there is some interest on her part in being more than just friends. Interest on her part arouses my interest. Then I am off to the races again. (*Laughter*)

Student: In a way you were rejecting her offer of friendship.

Student: I never had this before, and it's strange. I was telling Dr. Hora that I took it as a rejection and he said, "No, it's good." This is kind of a running conflict. What is her interest in me? And what is my interest in her?

Student: You just used the word "interest," and you are worried about her interest in you. What is it? So often when I'm concerned about what's going on, and I seek the meaning, I notice that I have a vested interest in a particular outcome. I just offer that because we are learning here that where our interest lies is the important thing in life.

Dr. Hora: Where our interest lies, that's where our lies are. (*Laughing*) We are lying to ourselves and we are lying to others. That is called "relationships".

Student: If I were in his shoes, I might think it a compliment that someone would like to know me not for sex but as a friend—for some spiritual reason. I think it would be wonderful, a revelation.

Dr. Hora: That's a very good point. Right. What you take as a rejection, she understands as a beautiful compliment. It's a very good point.

Student: I think that in this dating thing, a lot of women say, "You're not interested in me for myself. I am just sort of an object or something."

Student: Just an escort. That thought comes to me, too. She just sees me as an escort. She has nothing to do on Saturday night or Sunday afternoon, so she'll go out with me and have a nice afternoon. (*Laughing*)

Student: Isn't it interesting that we all speak a different language. It seems that in this world, everyone seems to be speaking a different language. Sounds like we are really in Babel[5] when it comes to this conversation.

Dr. Hora: The tower of Babel. When they were building the tower, they couldn't communicate. And indeed, in life it happens to peoplewho pretend and who have different motivations and language and misunderstandings. There are always conflicts and disappointments. That is what movies are made of.

---

5 - *See* Genesis 11:1-7

Student: Sometimes it's helpful, when you find yourself thinking these kinds of thoughts, you can label it for what it is: an interpersonal, interactive thought, and say, "I am going to refuse. I am not going to think this way." We need to recognize that non-personal, non-conditional benevolence is the issue. If we are really interested in that and we are sincere about it, all of these thoughts will be wiped away. That's real love, because it is of God. Who knows what effect that will have?

Dr. Hora: Sometimes people marry in ignorance with a secret fantasy of some kind of companionship of a shared interest, but as the years go by they grow in different directions. One of them is interested in sex. The other may be interested in power or money or something else. Since there was never a sincere companionship to begin with, they really live secret lives and they are departing further and further from each another and they don't know it, and they keep it a secret. It is very sad because they live together. They share a bed. They share the table, but they have secrets. They live secret lives, and that is a very sad thing. Many people live that way. They cannot share each other's values and fantasies because they each have their own modes of being in the world. Outwardly it looks like a marriage and even like a family, but actually it is a secret. Everybody is living his own secret. Now, in Metapsychiatry we say, "Discretion shall preserve thee, understanding shall save thee, compassion shall heal thee, but secretiveness can destroy thee." Companionship is primary. It is a first step if we are sincere about getting into a good marital life and a family life. There cannot be any secrets.

Student: When you say "secrets," do you mean secret fantasies and thoughts about how life should be?

Dr. Hora: Exactly. When you hear the word "companionship," take off your hat and take off your shoes, for you are standing on holy ground.[6] It is very important to appreciate companionship. It is the beginning of the good life.

Student: What do you mean by "companion?"

Dr. Hora: A companion is somebody whom you can respect and enjoy sharing ideas and values of your life. That is a companion.

Student: Does it have to be spiritual? Can you have good human companionship?

Dr. Hora: It is better than nothing. But the best is when the companionship is based on Christly values. I don't mean "church values" but *spiritual* values. You enjoy these values together, and you have endless opportunities to talk to each other and to clarify the thoughts. It is beautiful and very, very satisfying. A successful and happy marriage must be based on the idea of companionship. Without that, there is no marriage.

---

6 - "And he said, Draw not nigh hither: put off thy shoes from off thy feet, for the place whereon thou standest is holy ground." (Exodus 3:5)

8

Perfection

Student: We have talked a number of times about perfection and that there is no such thing as "personal perfection." I believe that's true, but I don't really understand that that's true. How can I really understand that I cannot do anything perfectly, I cannot be perfect, and that perfection is just not possible on the human level?

Dr. Hora: Well, is there such a thing as "perfection," in general?

Student: Yes. The idea that is needed for a particular problem in a particular point and time is the perfect idea, and then when that comes to us it's a great blessing.

Dr. Hora: What happens when such a perfect idea finds us and expresses itself as a perfect accomplishment? What happens? We know there are many, many works in the world, especially works of art, science, and poetry that express perfection. So what are we talking about? I think we have spoken about the difference between "perfection" and "perfectionism." Many Zen masters are constantly practicing Japanese calligraphy with a brush and ink. What are they doing? Just playing? No, they are trying to catch perfection. They are interested in those moments when God is coming through their consciousness and whatever they do, happens to be perfect.

Student: In, *Zen in the Art of Archery*[1], when the student hits a bull's eye, the student says, "Let us bow to perfection."

1 - *Zen in the Art of Archery*, by Eugen Herrigel, 1948.

Dr. Hora: "Let us bow to perfection." So, there *is* perfection. What is good about it is that it heals us of perfectionism. Is perfectionism a sickness?

Student: Yes.

Dr. Hora: You know that. And in some people it can become an obsession.

Student: Yes, I know that too. (*Laughter*)

Dr. Hora: It's a torture, yes, because we cannot produce perfection. If we try, we are neurotic and we suffer from a neurotic disease which is called "perfectionism." The Zen master, when he is practicing with brush and ink, he is preparing himself for the eventuality that perhaps, one of these days, when he is painting some character, it will be perfect.

Student: How does he know that it is perfect?

Dr. Hora: How does he know? Well, it is hard to answer, but it is possible to know. It's flawless. A piece of work can be flawless, and we know it. (*Addressing a student who is a dress desig*ner) If you design a garment and it is flawless, you know it. There is a great sense of release and even gratitude that God has chosen you as a medium through which He is expressing His perfection. For whatsoever God doeth, is perfect. Nothing shall be put to it nor taken away from it.[2] That's the way you can know.

Student: What does "perfectionism" mean?

---

2 - "I know that, whatsoever God doeth, it shall be forever: nothing can be put to it, nor any thing taken from it..." (Ecclesiastes 3:14)

Dr. Hora: Perfectionism is an arrogant approach to whatever we are doing that willfully pursues the ability to produce a piece of perfect work. It is very painful and unnerving.

Student: How do we lose interest in perfectionism if we have been taught that we can be humanly perfect?

Dr. Hora: It is not possible humanly. Whenever it happens, it is divine; it is not human.

Student: So how do we become perfect? If we only *believe* that perfection does exist, how does one *understand* that it exists? I mean, there is a belief, but we have to get acquainted with perfection.

Dr. Hora: Yes. Well, in Zen they have such a thing as training themselves to allow perfection to appear, and they have the method of practicing calligraphy. That is a good practice. And we were reminded about the art of archery. They practiced this archery day and night for who knows how long.

Student: How, in practical life, can these ideas be applied? Like when going to work?

Dr. Hora: It is not applied. It happens to you. When you pursue perfection in your activities, you are preparing your consciousness to be in tune with the possibility of allowing something perfect to appear. Personal intentionality has no place in it.

Student: Is that true, even if we are conscientious? Because, sometimes when I am at work as a teacher, it will happen that the idea for a particular lesson or activity just works out perfectly. The activity is good, the timing works out, all the kids are interested, they are all attentive, they all seem to learn, and I can tell that it was the manifestation of perfection. Other times, even though I would like it to be good, it's not terrible, but I have the nagging feeling afterwards that something could have been better.

Dr. Hora: Yes, right.

Student: And so I will try to improve it.

Dr. Hora: We cannot be personally perfect. The harder we try, the worse it gets.

Student: I guess what the whole thing seems to boil down to is motivation. Because if our motivation is in any way willful, if there is any desire for self-confirmation, then we can't. So we have to somehow, in every aspect of our lives, seek the right idea, which in this case would be understanding what "perfect" means.

Dr. Hora: Yes. Let go and let God. Now, suppose we would like to catch a beautiful young lady? (*Laughter*) She seems to be perfection itself. Right? But she is not interested. You know the story about Nasruddin who traveled the whole world looking for the perfect wife and could never find the perfect woman. One day he was in Cairo, Egypt, and he finally found the perfect woman. Very elated, he rushed to his friends and said, "Finally I found the perfect woman," and the friends said, "That's wonderful!" He said, "It's not so wonderful: I asked her to marry me, and she said, "No, I am looking for the perfect man." (*Laughter*)

Now, in so called "human relationships," there are situations where we are trying very hard to be involved in a very pleasant, intelligent conversation, and we think it is very important, because if we can communicate in a pleasant way, then something good can come out of it. And if you try to be a perfect conversationalist and have perfect responses to a situation, you will find you will always put your foot in your mouth. (*Laughter*) There are some people who always do that and always get rejected. The harder they try to be easy-going, knowledgeable conversationalists the more they put their feet in their mouths. What is going on here? How can you become a perfect companion and communicate perfectly?

Student: You have to have the right motivation.

Dr. Hora: Exactly. Surely.

Student: You have to be interested in harmonious coexistence.

Dr. Hora: Exactly. Harmonious "people" are not interested really in harmonious coexistence. They always want to prove something. To show something or to influence somebody, or make something good happen. Suppose you are an artist and you want to make a perfect piece of art. If you have in your mind that you are going to produce this, it won't work. So the Zen master says, "Erase yourself utterly." Now, what does that mean?

Student: We have to lose interest in self-confirmation.

Dr. Hora: All self-confirmatory motivations have to disappear, and God's will must have the free flow of manifesting itself. That's perfection. You see, with creativity you don't have to be some special kind of artist or scientist or inventor, you just have the right motivation, and the creative process is allowed to happen.

When you watch some of the TV talk shows, what do you see? People are forever drowning each other in their words. Simultaneously two or three people will talk and force an issue trying to be heard, and it is impossible. Everybody is willful. Most of the time when people talk to each other, they are willful. They want to press their own viewpoint and suppress other people. They can't wait for the others to stop talking so that they can put in their five cents worth of ideas.

In Zen training in Japan there is a custom for a student, when he comes for a private session with the Zen master, to prostrate himself in front of the master and touch the ground with his forehead. This is *dokusan*, a particular form of private session between the student and the master. If you don't do it right, you can be reprimanded. What could be the meaning? Are these masters so vain they demand this tremendous expression of respect? For us in our culture, it is humiliating to bow down before another human being. Right? Have you ever heard about this custom of obeisance, in which the student of Zen has to bow down all the way before he can exchangesome words with the master? What is the meaning of this?

Student: He is giving up his personal way of bowing down. There is only one way to do it, right?,

Dr. Hora: How do you know that there is only one way? Maybe there are two ways.

Student: Well, if he is doing it the wrong way, there must be....

Dr. Hora: We asked what the meaning is of this unusual custom. It is seemingly a humiliating custom.

Student: Is it to teach one to be humble?

Dr. Hora: Well, it could be that, but you see, the issue is to achievea situation of perfect communication. If you have in your heart such great respect for the activity of this Zen master, this unusually enlightened man, you are not going to get into a conversational jam with him. You are acknowledging first of all his spirituality, second of all great knowledge, and you are willing to be grateful for his teaching. When you have these proper thoughts about the man, your conversation will be as Jesus said, "Yea, yea or nay, nay."[3] There is nothing more to be said. And this is a perfectly harmonious conversation and exchange of thoughts. Isn't it interesting? There are no arguments, there is no shouting your ideas and debating and arguing and waiting for the moment when they catch their breath to insert your ideas to confirm yourself. Nobody is confirming.

Somebody asked, "Isn't that silly for a man to bow down before another man?" And the Zen master said, "When a student bows down, he is not bowing down to a man, he is bowing down to God in this man." He is reverently expressing his deep appreciation and respect for that consciousness which has reached such a level of enlightenment. When he has this proper appreciation, he doesn't feel humiliated. He finds this a very holy, sacred moment of perfection of two individuals honoring God in the form of this bowing down. So, you don't hear those conversations where people are just beating each other over the head and fighting over who is right or who is wrong. It is very interesting, because if you look at the values of our culture, it would seem that you are just humiliating yourself by bowing down and allowing the master to say something. But it is perfect harmony. The whole situation is consecrated to the spirit of God. This positive regard is for each other, for the Truth of Being. It is very good, but if we don't understand it, it seems ridiculous.

I heard a story about an astrophysicist in Princeton. He was giving a lecture about astrophysics — a very hard, specialized lecture, and after the lecture was over, a lady came up to him and said, "Professor, I enjoyed your lecture very much and I want you to know that I like

---

3 - "But let your communication be, Yea, yea; Nay, nay: for whatsoever is more than these cometh of evil." (Matthew 5:37)

it and I agree with you completely." And the professor said, "Lady, I spit on you, too." These are cultural differences in East and West.

Do you know the perfect art of spitting at people? That's perfection.

Student: I missed that. I don't understand what that means.

Dr. Hora: Spitting. You don't know what that means?

Student: That statement you just made. I don't get it.

Dr. Hora: Oh, you don't get it. Who else didn't get it? Nobody got it. When you say to somebody, "I agree with you," you are spitting on him.

Student: You are saying, "I know what you know."

Dr. Hora: "And I know even more."

Student: And he has raised himself to a certain level, and there she is, putting herself in his place.

Dr. Hora: The Zen master says, "Don't agree and don't disagree." In many families, clubs, and organizations, people are constantly agreeing and disagreeing. It generates hostility. If you agree, you condescend; if you disagree, you are insulting, right?

[The recording of the session ends here.
The remaining segment of the class was not recorded.]

Other books by Thomas Hora, M.D.

═══ ═══

For more information about Metapsychiatry visit:
www.PAGL.org

www.ingramcontent.com/pod-product-compliance
Lightning Source LLC
Chambersburg PA
CBHW061830040426
42447CB00012B/2901